The
Labyrinth of
Capital Gains
Tax Policy

The
Labyrinth of
Capital Gains
Tax Policy

A Guide for the Perplexed

Leonard E. Burman

BROOKINGS INSTITUTION PRESS

Washington, D.C.

ABOUT BROOKINGS

The Brookings Institution is a private nonprofit organization devoted to research, education, and publication on important issues of domestic and foreign policy. Its principal purpose is to bring knowledge to bear on current and emerging policy problems. The Institution maintains a position of neutrality on issues of public policy. Interpretations or conclusions in publications of the Brookings Institution Press should be understood to be solely those of the authors.

Copyright © 1999
THE BROOKINGS INSTITUTION
1775 Massachusetts Avenue, N.W., Washington, D.C. 20036
www.brookings.edu

Library of Congress Cataloging-in-Publication data
Burman, Leonard.
    The labyrinth of capital gains tax policy : a guide for the perplexed /
Leonard E. Burman.
        p.   cm.
    Includes bibliographical references and index.
    ISBN 0-8157-1270-7 (alk. paper)
    ISBN 0-8157-1269-3 (pbk.: alk. paper)
    1. Capital gains tax—United States. I. Title.
    HJ4653.C3 B874 1999   99-6203
    336.24'3dc2   CIP

9 8 7 6 5 4 3 2 1

The paper used in this publication meets minimum requirements of the American National Standard for Information Sciences—Permanence of Paper for Printed Library Materials: ANSI Z39.48-1984.

Typeset in Sabon

Composition by R. Lynn Rivenbark
Macon, Georgia

Printed by R. R. Donnelley and Sons
Harrisonburg, Virginia

To my parents, Max and Kathy Burman

Labyrinth, *also called maze, system of intricate passageways and blind alleys. . . . The task is to get to the center, marked in some conspicuous way, then to return; but even those who know the key are apt to be perplexed. Sometimes the design consists of alleys only, with no center.*

—THE NEW ENCYCLOPAEDIA BRITANNICA (1995)

PREFACE

Capital gains have been taxed in the United States since the enactment of the individual income tax in 1913. For that entire time span, controversy has surrounded the question of how such gains should be taxed. This book examines the current taxation of capital gains in the context of historical experience in the United States and compares it with the systems in other countries. The larger purpose is to determine how capital gains differ from other forms of income and how taxing capital gains affects saving, the federal budget, and economic growth.

This work began when I was at the Congressional Budget Office (CBO). Some parts have already been published as CBO reports, but others are seeing the light of day for the first time. Throughout the writing I have benefited from the advice and assistance of many people. My former supervisors at the CBO, Rosemary Marcuss and Frank Sammartino, read and commented encouragingly on various drafts. Peter Ricoy collaborated on the work reported in chapter 6. Larry Ozanne read an earlier draft closely and checked it for accuracy. Jeff Groen, Richard Kasten, and David Weiner also contributed expert analysis and advice. Meta Brown, Chris Duquette, and Stephanie Weiner provided excellent research assistance. Many people gave me helpful comments and advice on the CBO drafts, including Jerry Auten,

Robert Dennis, Alfred Drummond, Fred Goldberg, Jane Gravelle, Arlene Holen, R. Glenn Hubbard, Benjamin Page, James Poterba, and George Zodrow. Sherwood Kohn edited the earlier version, assisted by Marlies Dunson. Simone Thomas, Denise Jordan, and Kathryn Quattrone provided extensive help with the mechanical details of the manuscript.

Through the generous support of the Urban Institute, I was able to expand this work into a book after I left the CBO. Norma Coe provided cheerful and competent research assistance. Theresa Plummer and Peggy McConkey helped me prepare the final manuscript. Mark Hoffenberg and Missie Burman read portions of it and offered helpful suggestions. Bill Gale, who read two drafts, provided cheerleading and redirection to keep the project on track. Joel Slemrod helped improve the book immeasurably through his meticulous review of the penultimate draft. Three anonymous reviewers also provided excellent suggestions. The editorial and production staff at Brookings—Jill Bernstein, Nancy Davidson, Tanjam Jacobson, Vicky MacIntyre, Janet Walker, and Susan Woollen—improved the book in a thousand ways and were a delight to work with.

Finally, I owe a special debt to my wife, Missie, and to my children, Rob, Paul, Kent, and Elizabeth, who were always remarkably patient and supportive, even when the project consumed many evenings and weekends that rightfully belonged to them.

The views expressed in this book are mine alone and should not be attributed to those who read and commented on earlier drafts, or to any of the institutions with which I have been affiliated. In the case of my current employer, the Department of the Treasury, an especially strong disclaimer is warranted. When new tax laws are enacted, companies are sometimes granted temporary exemptions from the new law on existing investments by transition rules. Treasury granted me a generous transition rule on this book—allowing me to publish it—because it had been completed but for editorial revisions before I accepted my new position. It is in no way a product of the Treasury Department, and nothing in it should be construed as a statement in my capacity as a government official.

CONTENTS

TABLES

FIGURES

THE NOT-SO-GREAT DEBATE

On January 28, 1992, President George Bush addressed a joint session of Congress in which he insisted that the government lower the tax on profits realized in the sale of assets, widely known as capital gains. For the fourth time in as many years, he was railing against the tax, and his frustration and passion were palpable: "This time, at this hour, I cannot take no for an answer. You must cut the capital gains tax on the people of our country. . . . A cut in the capital gains tax increases jobs and helps just about everyone in our country."[1]

To President Bush and other advocates of the cut, the issue was simple. Lower tax rates on capital gains would spur saving, generate economic growth, and create jobs, all at no cost to the Treasury. The president viewed those opposed to such cuts as cynics practicing class warfare who could not stand to see the well-heeled pay lower taxes, even when the whole economy gained. They reminded Bush of "the Puritan who couldn't sleep at night, worrying that somehow, someone somewhere was out having a good time." He complained to Congress that "the opponents of this measure and those who have authored various so-called soak-the-rich bills that are floating around this Chamber should be reminded of something: When they aim at the big guy, they usually hit the little guy."

Those on the other side of the debate felt just as passionately that lower tax rates on capital gains are simply a windfall for the rich, that in fact they are bad for the economy and bad for the budget. Robert McIntyre, director of the liberal advocacy group Citizens for Tax Justice, angrily denounced the Bush proposal:

> The evidence from the past is overwhelmingly clear: capital gains tax cuts have never been good for jobs or economic growth. . . . The Bush economic strategy of throwing tax breaks at the wealthy is a proven failure. We don't need more empty office buildings. We don't need to divert capital into wasteful tax shelters and away from its most productive uses. In short, we don't need to repeat the mistakes of the past.[2]

In 1992 the Congress narrowly sided with McIntyre.[3] Once again, President Bush was disappointed.

In 1997, four years after George Bush left office, a Republican Congress lowered the top rate on long-term capital gains from 28 percent to 20 percent. Many in Congress would like to reduce the rate still further. The debate rages on.

Navigating the Labyrinth

So what drives the zealots on both sides of the debate? In a word, it is statistics. The trouble is, the statistical evidence many find convincing is actually deeply flawed. To make matters worse, some are satisfied to rest their case on anecdotal evidence. Further complicating matters, some disregard one of the basic principles of public finance, the theory of second best, which states that one element of an "ideal" tax system is not necessarily by itself an improvement when married to a necessarily imperfect system.

This book lays out what I have learned about capital gains in my research. Its aim is to attack the shibboleths about capital gains and replace them with facts and an accurate assessment of the evidence of their economic effects. Armed with that evidence, policymakers and analysts will recognize that the key to navigating the labyrinth of capital gains tax policy lies in the principles of public finance: efficiency, equity, and simplicity.

In practice, efficiency in the realm of public finance amounts to interfering as little as possible with well-functioning markets, while designing taxes or subsidies to move consumption and production toward efficient levels in markets that fail to meet the conditions for efficiency. Because the conditions for efficiency are often difficult to identify in imperfect markets, the logical response is to strive for neutrality—that is, to tax different forms of income in the same way—unless there is convincing evidence of a market failure that can be addressed through the tax system.

Tax equity requires that people be taxed according to their ability to pay. This principle rests on two assumptions. The first is that people with equal ability to pay should pay the same tax. Economists call this notion "horizontal equity." The second is that people with greater ability to pay should pay more tax. This is called "vertical equity." Some would also add that those with greater ability should pay a larger share of their incomes than those with lesser ability. This belief underlies the progressivity of marginal rates in the income tax.

The costs to the government in administering a tax and to individuals and businesses in complying with it are a loss to society. Under a simple tax system, few of society's resources have to be allocated to the unproductive activity of tax compliance, and more are available to produce valuable goods and services. If it is hard to enforce a tax or monitor a subsidy, aggressive or dishonest taxpayers may receive more tax benefit than others. This violates horizontal equity.

More than most other aspects of tax policy, decisions pertaining to capital gains involve sharp trade-offs among the different principles. These trade-offs explain why intellectually honest and well-informed people can come to different conclusions about the proper tax treatment of capital gains. For example, I would rank equity and simplicity high among the basic principles. Others would give greater weight to efficiency. And, as already mentioned, some people rely on evidence that I consider to be flawed.

Because I believe that capital gains should be taxed like other forms of income, at least when tax rates are relatively low, I start by laying out the contrary argument: the evidence shows that low tax rates on capital gains advance all three public finance objectives.

The Argument for Preferential Tax Treatment of Capital Gains

At present, capital gains on assets held at least a year (long-term capital gains) are highly favored over other kinds of income. Capital gains are only taxed when "realized" in the form of cash income. In other words, capital gains taxes may be deferred indefinitely by the simple expedient of holding an asset rather than selling it. Moreover, capital gains on assets held until death or donated to charity are never taxed. Thus, even without a preferential tax rate, capital gains would be treated more favorably than other returns to capital such as interest and dividends, which are taxed annually.

Under the Tax Reform Act of 1986 (TRA86), capital gains were to be taxed at the same rates as other income (up to a top rate of 28 percent). But in 1990 and 1993 the top rate on other income increased, while the top rate on capital gains was held fixed. That is how the rates on capital gains came to differ from those on other income. The Taxpayer Relief Act of 1997 reduced the top rate on long-term capital gains to a maximum of 20 percent, or half the top rate on ordinary income. The 1997 act also exempted almost all capital gains on residences.

What arguments persuaded the Congress to enrich the capital gains tax preference in 1997? Why do some members believe that the top rate should be cut further, to 15 percent or less? The answers to these questions lie in the notion that low rates are the historical norm where capital gains are concerned, that such rates promote national saving and investment and increase productivity, and that taxing capital gains is unfair.

The Historical Norm

Low tax rates on capital gains have been the historical norm in the United States and are the rule in the rest of the industrialized world.

Before TRA86 eliminated the rate preference for capital gains, 60 percent of long-term capital gains were excluded from taxable income. That is, the effective tax rate on capital gains was only 40 percent of the rate on other income. Capital gains were granted preferential status within ten years of the enactment of the modern income tax, and they retained that status in one form or another until 1986.

Most of the major trading partners of the United States tax capital gains at lower rates than other income. Several countries—notably Germany, the Netherlands, and Belgium—exempt long-term capital gains from tax altogether. Two countries—the United Kingdom and Australia—tax capital gains at full rates, but only after adjusting them for the effects of inflation. To the extent that lower rates on capital gains signal pro-saving tax policy, it should not be surprising that most developed countries have higher savings rates than the United States.

Positive Effect on Saving, Investment, and Productivity

Economists agree that the income tax penalizes saving. Cutting taxes on the returns to saving leads to more saving and investment and thus to higher economic growth. The best policy would be to exempt all saving from tax, as would be the case under a consumption tax, national retail sales tax, or flat tax. Cutting taxes on capital gains, which would be a first step toward a consumption tax, is a good place to start.

For one thing, cutting these taxes can actually increase tax receipts. Unlike taxes on other forms of income, the tax on capital gains is easy to avoid, by not selling assets or by following more complex strategies offered by financial advisers. Although Congress has passed many laws aimed at deterring tax avoidance, they are destined to fail as long as the tax rate on capital gains is high.

When the rate falls, however, taxpayers are more willing to sell assets in their portfolios. Moreover, fewer tax avoidance strategies are worthwhile at a tax rate of 15 percent than at a rate of 20 percent. For these reasons, cutting the tax rate on capital gains induces so many additional realizations that revenues increase over a large range of tax rates. Careful econometric studies published in top economic journals show that the "revenue-maximizing" rate for capital gains is less than 20 percent.[4]

Another benefit of reducing capital gains "lock-in" is that it gives taxpayers more incentive to diversify their portfolios so that they do not bear too much risk when assets change in value. Perhaps more important from a social perspective, they can sell assets that are over-valued and invest the proceeds in more promising ventures.

Capital gains merit special treatment because the kinds of assets that generate capital gains are different from other assets. Start-up businesses are most likely to be financed with equity and retain earn-ings to finance growth for many years before ever paying a dividend. That is, risky new ventures are most likely to pay all their returns in the form of capital gains. Society should encourage risk-taking, the kinds of investments that might produce the next Microsoft or Intel. Cutting the tax rate on capital gains encourages such investments. If they prove to be successful, the government still takes a share of the rewards, although it is much smaller. If they fail—new ventures are more likely to fail than established businesses—large capital losses are not deductible against other income. Thus taxing realized capital gains fully but allowing only limited deductibility of capital losses cre-ates an asymmetry that is especially damaging to risky investments. Reducing the tax rate on gains partly offsets this asymmetry.

Yet another point often mentioned is that capital gains on corporate stock are already taxed under the corporate income tax, so taxing them again amounts to a double tax. A 1992 Treasury study concludes that such double taxation can cause substantial distortions in the allocation of capital: too few businesses choose to incorporate and those that do are likely to avoid equity finance.[5] Many major trading partners of the United States allow shareholders a credit for corporate income taxes paid against taxes on dividends and capital gains on stock. Reducing or eliminating the tax on capital gains can have a similar effect.

An Unfair Tax

For many people, capital gains realizations are one-time events, rep-resenting income that has accrued over many years. Taxing families on the gain from the sale of a family business, for example, can make them appear to be rich even though they typically have quite modest incomes. Because income tax rates are progressive with income, a single large realization—if taxed like other income—could push a middle-income taxpayer into a very high tax bracket. This is unfair.

Thus the statistical evidence showing that almost all gains are realized by people with high incomes is misleading when income includes capital gains. In fact, half of the people who have capital gains have modest incomes. The rhetoric of the class warriors, which equates capital gains with wealth, is wrong.

It is also unfair to tax capital gains that simply represent inflation. Many small businesses are ultimately sold for less money in real terms than the owners had invested over the years. According to a 1997 study by the Congressional Budget Office (CBO), the average capital gain realized in 1993 from the sale of a business was actually a loss after correcting for inflation.[6] Such sales can nonetheless incur substantial capital gains tax liability.

Assessing the Arguments

This book examines these apparently compelling arguments. Chapter 2 reviews the complex laws governing the definition and taxation of capital gains, the history of capital gains taxation in America, the treatment of capital gains by the states, and the treatment in other parts of the world. Chapter 3 provides additional information on the assets that produce capital gains and how they do so.

In chapter 4, the discussion turns to the crucial question of how the taxation of capital gains affects saving and investment on both the private side (by altering the rate of return on capital gains assets) and on the public side (by providing an important source of revenues under the income tax). This question is surrounded by controversy in the economic literature and in the public debate. The chapter therefore pays special attention to the implications of economic research.

Lower tax rates on capital gains can affect productivity by directing capital investment to more or less efficient uses. The taxation of capital gains could improve economic efficiency by having an influence on whether people hold or sell assets, by encouraging or discouraging risk-taking and entrepreneurship, by offsetting or compounding the effects of the corporate income tax, by stimulating or deterring tax shelters, and by creating complexity and pushing up administrative costs. Chapter 5 weighs the evidence on each of these dimensions.

Much of the debate about capital gains has centered on fairness, examined in chapter 6. Are capital gains the province of the rich alone, or do many "little people" realize capital gains? Are the tabulations of capital gains by income misleading because people look rich when they realize an isolated capital gain? Can people with a high income avoid tax on capital gains more readily than others? How does inflation affect the picture?

Chapters 7 to 9 look at alternative ways of taxing capital gains. Economists tend to favor indexing for inflation because it causes income to be measured more accurately. The issue is complicated in the case of capital gains, for two reasons: capital gains are taxed only upon realization, and indexing gains when other forms of income and expense are unindexed can make the tax system less neutral with respect to inflation. Chapter 7 presents the pros and cons of indexing capital gains for inflation. Chapter 8 considers a number of options for altering the taxation of capital gains. And chapter 9 suggests some desirable reforms.

2

HOW CAPITAL GAINS
ARE TAXED

When the income tax was introduced in the United States, capital gains were taxed like other forms of income. Because the income tax applied only to people with high incomes, few capital gains were taxed, but when they were they could be subject to high rates. Taxpayers objected because a single transaction could represent years of deferred income, and the realization of a capital gain could push people who might not otherwise be taxable into very high tax brackets.[1] To deal with the problem, the Congress enacted an alternative rate on capital gains in the 1920s and kept the rate lower until the Tax Reform Act of 1986 (TRA86).

TRA86 dramatically lowered tax rates on ordinary income and reduced the number of tax brackets from eleven to three, but it also ended the practice of excluding a portion of long-term capital gains from income. Upon realization, capital gains were to be taxed at the full rates. Congress reasoned that a preferential rate was no longer necessary when the rates on ordinary income were low. But it also anticipated that the top income tax rate might increase in the future, so it capped the tax on capital gains at the top rate then, which was 28 percent. The cap became relevant in 1991 when tax rates on ordinary income increased. The top rates on ordinary income increased again in 1993, making the difference between the tax rate on capital gains and ordinary income about twelve percentage points for people with the highest taxable incomes.

Although there has been support in Congress for a reduction since 1986, the rate for most assets was not cut until the passage of the Taxpayer Relief Act of 1997 (TRA97). When fully phased in, this new law will tax most capital gains on assets held more than five years at a maximum rate of 18 percent; for assets held between one and five years, the maximum rate will be 20 percent. Special rules apply to sales of stock in small businesses, real estate, and collectibles such as jewelry and art.

Capital Gains Defined

For reasons that will shortly become apparent, the tax code takes hundreds of pages to define and limit what may be treated as a capital gain, but the basic idea is simple. A capital gain is the increase in value of a capital asset.[2] Although capital gains may accrue constantly over the life of an asset, they are included in taxable income only when an asset is sold, that is, when the gain is "realized" as cash income.[3] Capital gains on assets held until death or donated to charity are never realized in this sense and thus escape taxation altogether.

Assessing gains in terms of realized value is an intuitively sensible way to measure income, and it has a long history in English common law.[4] In Europe in the eighteenth and early nineteenth centuries, estates were typically entailed. That is, they were passed from generation to generation with the restriction that the lord, or life-tenant, had the rights to the income generated by the estate but could not sell the property. Thus increases or decreases in the value of the estate were not considered income because the owner had no right to tap it. That is said to be the basis for the realization principle underlying capital gains taxation.[5]

But this approach is problematic in the modern world and causes the tax laws to be very complex, unfair, and inefficient. Absent restrictions, taxpayers would have a strong incentive to convert all their capital income (as well as other income) into capital gains so as to postpone taxation until realization and then qualify for lower rates. To illustrate the complexity of the system, the interest on a bond is taxed as ordinary income as it is paid out, whereas any increase or decrease in value over time is generally considered a capital gain or loss and taxed only upon realization. An exception has to be made in the case of a "zero-coupon bond," which pays no interest. It is sold at a discount and pays all its return in the form of appreciation in value. There is no reason why the tax code should favor that form of bond over the kind that pays interest. Thus special rules impute taxable interest to such bonds. Another problem is that taxpayers with many capital assets can time the realization of gains and losses so as to pay little or no capital gains tax, even though they have large unrealized capital gains in their portfolios. In fact, were it not for limits on the deductibility of capital losses against other income, some taxpayers would be able to use the losses that are a normal part of large portfolios to shelter their other income from tax. Unfortunately, the necessary limitation on capital losses means that undiversified investors may pay substantial tax if their investment succeeds but get little tax benefit if it fails.

The realization principle also encourages investors to hold onto appreciated property to postpone paying tax. This "lock-in" effect is considered one of the main defects of the current system of taxing capital gains.[6] The lock-in effect is exacerbated by the nontaxation of capital gains at death, which provides an even bigger reward than mere postponement. Moreover, it has stimulated many schemes to allow people to gain access to the cash value of large investments without technically selling them. Those schemes have, in turn, led to complicated laws aimed at discouraging them.

Further problems arise because capital gains are defined in nominal terms; that is, they are not indexed for the effect of inflation. After accounting for inflation, the assets taxed are in many cases worth less when sold than the money invested. On one hand, this seems unfair, and it contributes to the riskiness of capital gains assets because of the possibility of unexpected inflation. On the other hand, the failure to index makes some sense in that other kinds of capital income are similarly affected by inflation and are also unindexed. Another point to consider is that inflation helps debtors more than it hurts those who have capital gains. Were gains indexed, but interest expense unindexed, investors could make a lot of money simply because of the asymmetry of tax treatment. Moreover, for reasons explained in chapter 7, indexing is especially problematic when gains are taxed upon realization.

Current Law

Under current law, nominal capital gain or loss (up to certain limits) is included in taxable income when an asset is sold. The Taxpayer Relief Act of 1997, as amended by the Internal Revenue Service (IRS) Restructuring and Reform Act of 1998, created a complicated web of special tax rates and rules for capital gains tailored to the type of asset and how long it has been held.[7] To limit the short-term revenue cost of the new law, some of the provisions will not take effect until 2000. When fully phased in, the law will tax most long-term capital gains at one of two rates: 18 percent for assets held more than five years; and 20 percent for assets held between one and five years. Gains on assets held less than a year (short-term gains) are taxed at the same rates as ordinary income. Long-term gains realized by taxpayers in the lowest tax bracket (15 percent) will be subject to a 10 percent rate if held from one to four years, and 8 percent if held for five years or more. The main features of current (1998) law are summarized in box 2-1.

Rate Structure

As just mentioned, the maximum tax rate for different assets depends not only on the type of asset and how long it is held, but also when it was bought. Short-term capital gains—on assets held less than one year—are taxed at the same rates as ordinary income (up to 39.6 percent). With a few exceptions, assets held longer than one year by taxpayers in the highest bracket (28 percent or higher) are currently taxed at a 20 percent rate; those in the 15 percent bracket face a maximum capital gains tax rate of 10 percent (see table 2-1).

Box 2-1. Salient Features of Capital Gains Taxation

—Tax rates for assets held longer than one year are generally lower than for other income, the maximum in most cases being 20 percent (18 percent for assets purchased after 2000 and held at least five years).

—Tax applies only when gains are realized and not at all for assets held until death. Heirs pay tax on the asset's value at the date of death (called a "step-up in basis").

—Capital gains on appreciated property donated to charity are generally not taxable.

—Net capital losses in excess of $3,000 may not be deducted against other income but may be carried over indefinitely to future years.

—Depreciable business investments qualify for preferential rates only to the extent that their gains are recaptured (exceed past depreciation deductions). Special rules and a 25 percent tax rate apply to nonrecaptured long-term capital gains on real estate.

—Most capital gains on home sales are exempt.

—Special rules apply to sales of stock in small businesses, exchanges of similar property, and gains on "collectibles."

—There is no explicit adjustment for the effects of inflation.

—Many other rules exist to deter capital gains tax avoidance and artificial conversion of ordinary income into preferentially taxed capital gains.

Starting in 2001, the rate on assets held more than five years will fall by two percentage points: to 18 percent for taxpayers in the upper bracket and 8 percent for those in the 15 percent marginal bracket. To qualify for the 18 percent rate (but not the 8 percent rate), an asset must have been purchased after 2000. As of January 1, 2001, taxpayers in the higher bracket may have their assets "marked to market." That is, they may pay tax on accumulated gains as if the assets had been sold and repurchased at their current fair market value.

Table 2-1. Capital Gains Tax Rates by Holding Period, Purchase Date, and Ordinary Income Tax Bracket (1998 Tax Law)ᵃ

Percent

Ordinary income tax bracket	Held < 1 year	Held 1–5 years	Sold before 2001	Held > 5 years	
				Sold after 2000ᵇ	
				Bought before 2001	Bought after 2000
15.0	15.0	10.0	10.0	8.0	8.0
28.0	28.0	20.0	20.0	20.0	18.0
31.0	31.0	20.0	20.0	20.0	18.0
36.0	36.0	20.0	20.0	20.0	18.0
39.6	39.6	20.0	20.0	20.0	18.0

a. Tax rate applying to gains on sales of assets other than collectibles and depreciable assets subject to recapture. See text.

b. Assets may be marked to market as of January 1, 2001, by paying tax on accrued capital gains. Marked-to-market assets are treated as if they had been purchased on January 1, 2001, and qualify for the lower top rate if held until 2006.

Assets that are marked to market in 2001 qualify for the lower tax rate on future gain if they are held at least five more years.

The system of maximum tax rates complicates income tax calculations. Taxpayers must do a separate rate calculation for each holding period and class of capital gain. The law recognizes two categories of holding period until 2001 and four thereafter (see table 2-1.) These calculations must be done twice for taxpayers who might be subject to the alternative minimum tax (AMT), because the maximum tax rates apply to the AMT as well as the regular income tax.[8] In the case of taxpayers whose ordinary income tax bracket would be 15 percent if they had no long-term capital gains but becomes 28 percent or higher when long-term capital gains are included, the portion of their capital gains that would be taxed at the 15 percent rate will have to be separated from the portion that would be taxed at higher rates and the appropriate maximum tax rates applied separately to each portion. Mutual funds will have to report capital gains in each of the four classes; before passage of the new law, they only had to report short- and long-term gains.

Taxpayers report capital gains and losses to the IRS on a Schedule D.[9] The 1998 version is reproduced in appendix A. Of the fifty-four lines on the schedule, the last thirty-six (lines 19 through 54) are devoted to the computation of maximum capital gains tax rates. The second page of the AMT tax form (not shown) performs similar calculations. Both of these tax forms will become even more complicated when the maximum tax rates for assets held five years or more become effective.

Collectibles (such as art, precious metals, and jewelry) held for one year or more are taxed at a maximum rate of 28 percent. (The last column of part II of the Schedule D is required to track gains taxed at this special rate.)

Short-term capital gains and losses are generally taxed at the same rates as ordinary income. Long-term capital gains realized by corporations are also fully taxable at the same rates as other income. The maximum corporate tax rate on capital gains is 35 percent. Like other forms of capital income and expense, the tax code makes no adjustment for the effects of inflation on the real (inflation-adjusted) returns from a capital investment. As a result, an asset being sold may be taxable even though, in real terms, it is worth less than when it was purchased.

Because different classes of capital gains and losses are taxed at different rates, taxpayers must net capital losses against capital gains within each class. For example, a taxpayer in the 36 percent bracket with both net long-term and net short-term gains is taxed at the 20 percent rate on the net long-term gains and at the 36 percent rate on the net short-term gains. If the taxpayer had net long-term gains in excess of net short-term losses, the difference would be taxed at the 20 percent (long-term gain) rate. If net short-term gains exceeded net long-term losses, the difference would be treated as a short-term gain and taxed at the 36 percent rate. If the net result of all gains and losses is a net loss, up to $3,000 of the net capital loss is deductible against other income, with the remainder (if any) being carried over to later tax years. The losses carried over retain their short- or long-term character according to another complicated set of rules. The treatment of losses will be further complicated when the special rates for assets held for five years or more take effect.

Effect of Phaseouts on Capital Gains Rates

In practice, marginal tax rates on capital gains may be much higher because of the effect of implicit tax surcharges created by tax benefits, such as the newly enacted child credit, that phase out with income.[10] For example, a couple with an adjusted gross income (AGI) of $100,000 and two children under the age of seventeen is in the phaseout range for the child credit. Every additional $1,000 of capital gain (or any other component of AGI), regardless of holding period, raises the couple's AGI by $1,000. But the additional $1,000 reduces the child credit by $50 (when it is fully phased in, in 1999). Thus the effective tax rate on capital gains increases by five percentage points. If the gain is subject to a direct capital gains tax of 20 percent, the phaseout of the child credit raises the effective tax rate to 25 percent (table 2-2 illustrates that calculation in more detail).

The effective tax rate on long-term capital gains may be as high as 43.8 percent because of the interaction with the partial taxation of social security benefits. In a certain range of income, every additional dollar of capital gain increases the taxable portion of social security by $0.85. At a 28 percent marginal tax rate, this increases tax liability by $0.238, or 23.8 percent of the capital gain (see table 2-3). Added to the 20 percent tax rate on long-term capital gains, that produces a 43.8 percent tax rate.

Most of the phaseouts and phase-ins do not affect the high-income taxpayers who realize most of the capital gains, but the phaseout of itemized deductions does. Joint returns with an AGI greater than $121,200 in 1997 lose $30 of itemized deductions for every $1,000 of additional income. That raises taxable income by $30; at the top marginal tax rate of 39.6 percent, the lost deductions cost the taxpayer $12 (39.6 percent of $30), or 1.2 percent of capital gains. Because itemized deductions (especially interest deductions and property taxes) tend to increase with income, that phaseout increases effective tax rates at all income levels above the floor. As a result, the tax rate on long-term capital gains for taxpayers with the highest incomes is really 19.2 percent (for assets held longer than five years and purchased after 2000) or 21.2 percent, rather than 18 percent and 20 per-

Table 2-2. Capital Gains Tax Calculation for Taxpayers in Phaseout for Child Credit[a]

Dollars

	Before gain	After gain	Change
Adjusted gross income (AGI)	100,000	101,000	1,000
Ordinary tax before credit	15,000	15,000	0
Capital gain	0	1,000	1,000
Capital gains tax (20 percent)	0	200	200
Total tax before credit	15,000	15,200	200
Child credit before limit	1,000	1,000	0
AGI: 90,000	10,000	11,000	1,000
Disallowed child credit	500	550	50
Allowable child credit	500	450	−50
Tax after credit	14,500	14,750	250
Change in tax as percent of gain	...	...	25

a. Example assumes joint return with two children under age seventeen, 1999 tax law.

cent, respectively. A similar calculation demonstrates that the phaseout raises the maximum effective tax rate on ordinary income from 39.6 percent to 40.8 percent.

Recapture of Depreciation

Capital gains on depreciable assets, such as business plant and equipment investments, must be treated differently to limit tax sheltering. Depreciation deductions are often accelerated, in the sense that the owner can deduct the cost of a machine or building faster than it actually wears out or declines in value. In general, if an asset is sold for more than its depreciated value (the purchase price less all the depreciation deductions claimed), the gain up to the amount of previous depreciation deductions is taxed as ordinary income, not as capital gain. That is, the past depreciation, which was deducted at ordinary income tax rates, is "recaptured": it is taxed at the same ordinary income rates. Only if the asset is sold for more than its purchase price is any portion of the gain taxed at the lower capital gains rates.

Special rules apply to real estate investments. Until passage of the Taxpayer Relief Act of 1997, gains on real estate were not recaptured as long as the investor had used the "straight-line" method of

Table 2-3. Marginal Tax Rate Surcharges Due to Phaseouts, 1997 Levels

Percent unless otherwise specified

Ordinary income tax bracket	Itemized deductions	Child credit[a]	Personal exemptions			Social security[b]	
			1	2	4	50	85
15.0	...	...	...	...	...	7.5	12.8
28.0	0.8	5	...	...	...	14.0	23.8
31.0	0.9	5	0.7	1.3	2.6	...	...
36.0	1.1	5	0.8	1.5	3.1	...	...
39.6	1.2		0.8	1.7	3.4	...	...
Range on joint returns (AGI, dollars)							
Beginning of range	121,200	90,000	181,800	181,800	181,800	32,000 - S/2	44,000 - S/2
Size of range	Large[c]	10,000 per child	125,000	125,000	125,000	S/2	S - 6,000 / .85

a. The child credit phaseout is at 1999 levels.

b. This is a phase-in rather than a phaseout. Taxpayers with "provisional income" (PI) above $32,000 pay tax on up to 50 percent of benefits, depending on income. Taxpayers with PI greater than $44,000 pay tax on up to 85 percent of benefits. PI is AGI plus tax-exempt interest, income earned abroad, and one-half of social security benefits. Both the beginning and size of the range depend on the amount of social security benefits (S).

c. For joint returns, itemized deductions are reduced by 3 percent of AGI above $121,200 in 1997, but the phased out amount is limited to 80 percent of allowable itemized deductions, excluding deductions for medical expenses, investment interest, and casualty, theft, or wagering losses. For example, if otherwise allowable itemized deductions are $20,000, the reduction is at most $16,000. This would correspond to an income range of $533,333. Since itemized deductions tend to increase with income, very few taxpayers are affected by the 80 percent limit.

depreciation. (That was the only option for real estate placed in service after 1986.) Only the excess of depreciation deductions over the value of straight-line depreciation was recaptured. The new law creates a special 25 percent tax rate for nonrecaptured real estate depreciation deductions. They are still taxed at lower rates than recapture gains on other kinds of depreciable assets, but not at rates as low as other capital gains.

Special Rules for Bequests and Gifts

Individuals can avoid paying tax on capital gains by holding the assets until death. The IRS does not assess a tax on the capital gains of assets held at death, and those who inherit appreciated assets use the value at the time of death as the basis for computing capital gain. That adjustment in basis is commonly referred to as "step-up in basis."

Capital gain or loss is not realized on gifts either, but the recipient of the gift must assume the basis of the donor for computing capital gain when the asset is sold. This treatment is called "carryover basis." Congress enacted a law applying carryover basis to bequests in 1976, effective the following year. In 1978 Congress retroactively delayed the effective date until 1980. In 1980 Congress reconsidered carryover basis yet again and decided to repeal it retroactively so it never actually took effect.[11]

The failure to tax capital gains at death is so notorious that it has been nicknamed "the angel of death loophole."[12] Economists estimate that as much as half of capital gains might escape taxation altogether because assets are held until death or donated to charity.

Many of the problems attributed to the taxation of capital gains may be traced to the angel of death loophole. For example, the most powerful incentive to hold onto appreciated assets (the lock-in effect) arises not because taxes may be deferred, but because they might be avoided altogether. Because the tax savings may be so great, taxpayers engage in a variety of complex financial techniques (discussed later) to extract cash from appreciated assets without realizing a capital gain for tax purposes. The cost of these stratagems contributes to the excess burden of the income tax (that is, the social cost of the tax in excess of the revenue it collects).

Other Special Provisions

Taxes on capital gains can also be avoided by donating appreciated assets to charity (subject to some limits). In general, a donation of appreciated property to a charitable organization is deductible at its current market value, rather than the taxpayer's cost. This effectively creates a double deduction for taxpayers, because they may deduct the full value of the property and they avoid paying the capital gains tax that they would have owed if they had sold the property first and then donated the proceeds to the charity. A taxpayer in the top income tax bracket might thus save 60¢ or more in federal and state taxes for every dollar donated in the form of appreciated property if most of its value represents capital gain.

Gains from sales of owner-occupied housing are largely exempt from tax because homeowners are allowed to exclude a gain of $500,000 ($250,000 if filing single) as long as the house was the primary residence for at least two of the last five years. Gains in excess of the exclusions are taxed in full at the applicable capital gains rate (depending on holding period and when the home was purchased). If a home is sold before it has been occupied for two years, the gain is included in taxable income unless the move was precipitated by a job change, poor health, or other unforeseen circumstances. In those special cases, the exclusion is reduced for each month under twenty-four months of occupancy on a pro rata basis. For example, if a single taxpayer moves to another city to take a job after living in a home for twelve months, the amount of gain that may be excluded from income is $125,000, rather than $250,000.

Gains on sales of stock held for at least five years in certain small businesses (with assets less than $50 million, engaged in a qualifying trade or business) qualify for a special tax rate of 14 percent. (Obviously, electing that tax rate would only be advantageous to taxpayers who would face a tax rate of 18 percent or higher on the capital gain.) The Taxpayer Relief Act of 1997 allows taxpayers to roll over the gain on stock in a small business held for at least six months if the proceeds are invested in other qualifying small business stock within sixty days of the sale. The gain from the original sale can then qualify for the special rate upon the sale of the replacement stock.

Exchanges of certain investment property are not treated as realization events when the exchanged property is similar or "like-kind." For example, exchanges are generally considered like-kind when they are in the same class for depreciation purposes. Stock in trade and financial assets, such as stocks and bonds, do not qualify as like-kind exchanges. Most real estate exchanges qualify as like-kind, and brokers provide matchmaking services to allow people to trade real estate without paying tax. Combined with the nontaxation of capital gains at death, this provision allows taxpayers to totally escape paying tax on the disposition of large real estate holdings as long as they hold the replacement asset until death (or exchange that for another property).

Anti–Tax Shelter Provisions

Individuals may deduct up to $3,000 in net capital losses (capital losses in excess of capital gains) in a single year. Individuals may use capital losses to offset capital gains in future years, subject to restrictions. Were it not for the loss limit, taxpayers with large diversified portfolios (which almost always contain some assets with losses) could realize losses, but defer gains, so as to shelter much of their ordinary income from tax liability. In addition, if losses could be fully deducted from other income, a taxpayer could stagger the realization of losses and gains so that the losses would all be deductible at rates as high as 39.6 percent, whereas the gains would be taxed only at the 18 or 20 percent rates.

Suppose Bill Smith purchased $700,000 worth of stock in Apple Computer and the same amount of stock in Intel in 1991. Apple struggled between 1991 and 1998, whereas Intel soared. In the fall of 1998, Bill Smith's stake in Apple was worth about $350,000, but his stake in Intel was worth about $8.7 million. Overall, his portfolio of tech stocks increased in value by $7.65 million, which amounts to a return of more than 30 percent a year. Nonetheless, without limits on losses, Bill could sell his Apple stock and reduce his taxable income by $350,000, saving as much as $138,600 in taxes in 1998 (39.6 percent of $350,000), despite the fact that his portfolio has done very well. Suppose he also wanted to sell 5 percent of his holding in Intel, realizing a gain of $400,000. If he did that in 1998, he would have paid $10,000 in tax (20 percent) on his net gain of $50,000. If he waited until the beginning of 1999 and there were no limits on losses, he would pay $80,000 in tax in 1999, reducing his net tax liability in the two years by $58,600, even though the transactions taken together produced a gain![13]

There are numerous other special tax provisions related to capital gains. Many are intended to prevent taxpayers from artificially converting ordinary income into capital gains and to limit arbitrage transactions that would take advantage of the difference between the tax rates on ordinary income and capital gains. By limiting the deductibility of interest, TRA86 restrains the ability of taxpayers to borrow and fully deduct the interest so as to finance investments that produce lightly taxed capital gains. The act prohibited the deductibility of consumer interest and limited the deduction of investment interest to the amount of investment income. If investment interest expense exceeds the amount of investment income apart from capital gains, it offsets capital gains dollar for dollar. That has the effect of limiting the value of investment interest deductions to the capital gains tax rate.

The tax law was recently amended in an effort to prevent a class of transactions that allow taxpayers to extract the gain from an appreciated asset without actually recognizing a gain for tax purposes. In the most notorious of these, called "short-against-the-box," a taxpayer who owns appreciated stock borrows shares in the same company and sells them instead of the stock he or she owns. That transaction extracts most of the cash value of the asset without generating any taxable gain. The shares are repaid after the taxpayer dies. Since gains are not taxable at death, that scheme effectively skirted capital gains tax liability altogether. The Taxpayer Relief Act of 1997 changed the rules so that such a transaction would be deemed a sale and gain would be recognized. Other gimmicks are still legal, though.

Recent History

Before TRA86 took effect, 60 percent of net long-term capital gains were excluded from an individual's taxable income. Thus, even though the top tax rate on ordinary income of 50 percent was higher than it is currently, the maximum effective tax rate on capital gains was the same 20 percent that it is now. The holding period for long-term status was shorter, at six months.

The decision in 1986 to tax capital gains at the same rate as ordinary income was a result of many compromises. The House of Representatives had proposed to retain a partial exclusion for long-term capital gains, but at less than the 60 percent rate then in effect. Thus the top effective tax rate on capital gains would remain close to 20 percent as marginal tax rates on ordinary income were cut. The House bill would have phased down the exclusion to 44 percent, yielding a top effective tax rate of 22 percent at the proposed top statutory tax rate of 38 percent.[14] The Senate proposed a further reduction in the maximum tax rate on ordinary income to 27 percent.

The report of the Senate Finance Committee argued that as long as ordinary income was taxed at that low level, an exclusion for capital gains was an unnecessary complication.[15] The exclusion was to be repealed primarily to simplify the income tax code. In addition, although it was not reflected in the committee's report, the higher tax rate on capital gains was offered in part as a compromise in order to obtain support for generally lower tax rates on the incomes of high-income taxpayers.[16]

The final bill, passed overwhelmingly by both houses of the Congress and signed by President Ronald Reagan, repealed the exclusion for capital gains but capped the tax rate at 28 percent, so that capital gains would not be taxed at higher rates if subsequent legislation raised income tax rates. In fact, the top effective tax rate on capital gains was substantially higher—33 percent—for taxpayers whose incomes fell in the so-called bubble created by the phaseout of the 15 percent rate bracket and personal exemptions in TRA86.

The Omnibus Budget Reconciliation Act of 1990 removed the bubble and raised the top tax rate on ordinary income to 31 percent while retaining a top tax rate of 28 percent on capital gains, although the phaseout of itemized deductions made the top effective tax rate somewhat higher (see the earlier section "Effect of Phaseouts on Capital Gains Rates").

The Omnibus Budget Reconciliation Act of 1993 raised the top tax rate still further to 39.6 percent, but the rate on capital gains remained capped. After 1993 the maximum effective tax rate on long-term capital gains (29.2 percent) was higher than the capital gains tax rates in any previous period except for 1970–78 (see table 2-4). In that period, the combination of high marginal tax rates on ordinary income and interactions between the capital gains tax and other tax provisions raised the top effective tax rate on long-term capital gains to almost 50 percent (although very few people were actually subject to such high rates). In addition, the difference between the tax rates on capital gains and other income between 1987 and 1997 was smaller than at any previous time, although it has increased because tax rates on ordinary income have increased. The 29.2 percent maximum tax rate on long-term capital gains effectively excluded about 30 percent of such gains from tax for the highest-income taxpayers.

By comparison, exclusions of 50 percent to 60 percent had been in effect between World War II and the passage of TRA86. In the 1950s and 1960s, capital gains were subject to an "alternative tax" that made the effective exclusion even larger. From 1954 to 1963, for example, the maximum marginal tax rate on ordinary income was 91 percent, but the maximum tax rate on capital gains was only 25 percent.

Not long after the enactment of TRA86, the Congress considered proposals to restore a tax preference for capital gains. President George Bush proposed to cut the capital gains tax rate in each of his four budgets.[17] The 1989 administration proposal would have imposed a maximum tax rate of 15 percent on capital gains on assets other than timber, real estate, and collectibles. In that year, House Ways and Means Committee chairman Dan Rostenkowski (Democrat of Illinois) proposed indexing capital gains for inflation. The committee passed another bill, introduced by Representatives Ed Jenkins (Democrat of Georgia), Ronnie G. Flippo (Democrat of Alabama), and Bill Archer (Republican of Texas) that would have allowed a

30 percent exclusion for assets sold before 1992, and indexing thereafter. The Congress did not enact any of these bills.

In 1990 President Bush proposed to exclude from taxable income 30 percent of the capital gain on most capital assets held more than three years. Gains on assets held for two years would qualify for a 20 percent exclusion and assets held for one year would qualify for a 10 percent exclusion. Gains on assets held for three or more years by high-income individuals would have been taxed at a rate of 19.6 percent (70 percent of 28 percent). The House passed a $1,000 annual exclusion and a 50 percent exclusion for gains above $1,000 up to a lifetime maximum. The Senate did not take up the bill. Tax rates on capital gains remained at 28 percent as part of the Omnibus Budget Reconciliation Act of 1990, which raised the tax rate on ordinary income for high-income taxpayers from 28 percent to 31 percent.

In 1991 Bush proposed a 30 percent exclusion again, but the Congress failed to act on it. In 1992 he proposed a 45 percent exclusion for assets held more than two years. Assets held for one or two years would have qualified for 15 percent and 30 percent exclusions, respectively. The House passed a tax bill (H.R. 4210) that, among other provisions, would have indexed newly acquired assets for inflation. The Senate version of H.R. 4210 would have provided a larger cut in capital gains tax rates to individuals in the lowest rate bracket and no tax cut to individuals in the highest bracket. The Congress adopted the Senate capital gains tax cut in the final version of the bill. President Bush vetoed the legislation, despite the capital gains tax cut, because of other provisions in the bill.

In 1993 President Bill Clinton proposed, and the Congress passed, a 50 percent exclusion for capital gains on certain small business stock acquired by individuals at original issue and held at least five years.[18] The Balanced Budget Act of 1995, passed by Congress but vetoed by Clinton, would have given individuals a 50 percent exclusion for all gains and losses and would have phased in indexing for long-term gains and losses on corporate stock, tangible business property, and personal residences. The 28 percent maximum tax rate on long-term capital gains would have been repealed. The 50 percent exclusion would have effectively reduced the maximum rate on capital gains

Table 2-4. Summary of Tax Treatment of Long-Term Capital Gains, 1913–97

Percent unless otherwise specified

| Years | Maximum marginal tax rate on ordinary income | Maximum tax rate on capital gains for high-income taxpayers | | Exclusion ratio for long-term capital gains | Holding period for long-term gains (years) |
		Statutory tax rate (net of exclusion)	Effective tax rate[a]		
1913–21	7–77	7–77	7–77	0	…
1922–33	24–73	12.5	12.5	50	2.0
1934–37	63–79	18.9–23.7	18.9–23.7	20–70	1.0[b]
1938–41	79–81.1	15.0	15.0	33–50	1.5[b]
1942–51	82–94	25.0	25.0	50	0.5
1952–53	92.0	26.0	26.0	50	0.5
1954–63	91.0	25.0	25.0	50	0.5
1964–67	70–77	25.0	25.0	50	0.5
1968	75.3	26.9	26.9	50	0.5
1969	77.0	27.5	27.5	50	0.5
1970	71.8	30.2	32.3	50	0.5
1971	70.0	32.5	38.8	50	0.5
1972–75	70.0	35.0	45.5	50	0.5
1976	70.0	35.0	49.1	50	0.5
1977	70.0	35.0	49.1	50	0.75
1978[c]	70.0	33.8	49.1	50	1.0

1979–80	70.0	28.0	28.0	50	1.0
1981[d]	70.0	20.0	20.0	50	1.0
1982–83	50.0	20.0	20.0	60	1.0
1984–86	50.0	20.0	20.0	60	0.5
1987	38.0	28.0	28.0	0	1.0
1988–90[e]	28.0	28.0	28.0	0	1.0
1991–92[f]	31.9	28.0	28.9	0	1.0
1993–96[f]	40.8	28.0	29.2	0	1.0
1997[f,g]	40.8	20.0	21.2	0	1.5
1998[f,h]	40.8	20.0	21.2	0	1.0

Source: Department of the Treasury, Office of the Secretary of the Treasury, Office of Tax Analysis, *Report to the Congress on the Capital Gains Tax Reductions of 1978* (September 1985), updated by the author.

a. Includes interactions with other tax provisions.

b. From 1934 to 1941 the exclusion ratio increased with holding period.

c. In 1978 the exclusion was increased from 50 percent to 60 percent for transactions occurring after October 31, 1978, thus reducing the maximum rate from 35 percent to 28 percent for taxpayers paying the ordinary income rate and to 34.9 percent for those paying the ordinary, minimum, and maximum rate.

d. In 1981 the maximum rate on capital gains was reduced from 28 percent to 20 percent for gains realized after June 9, 1981.

e. These rates apply to taxpayers with very high incomes. A higher 33 percent tax rate applied both to ordinary income and to capital gains for taxpayers in the "bubble" income range: the range in which the benefit of exemptions and of the 15 percent tax bracket were phased out.

f. These rates include the effects of section 68 of the Internal Revenue Code, which reduces the allowable itemized deductions by 3 percent of adjusted gross income above $100,000 (indexed for inflation after 1991). This limitation affects most high-income taxpayers. In addition, higher rates apply in the new bubble range, depending on family size. The phaseout of the child credit (starting in 1998) and the phase-in of taxation of social security can cause effective tax rates for some middle- and upper-middle-income taxpayers to be much higher than the rates shown (see table 2-3).

g. A 28 percent rate applied to assets held between one year and eighteen months.

h. An 18 percent rate will apply to assets purchased after 2000 and held for at least five years.

and losses to 19.8 percent. The exclusion would have applied to assets sold after tax year 1994; indexing would have applied to qualifying assets purchased after 2000. Personal residences would have been indexed for inflation occurring after 2000. The act would also have capped the tax rate on capital gains realized by corporations at 28 percent and would have allowed individuals to deduct capital losses on their homes against other income.

The Taxpayer Relief Act of 1997 made many changes to the way capital gains are taxed. It imposed new lower maximum tax rates on capital gains held at least eighteen months and introduced exemptions that would protect most homeowners from a capital gains tax on their homes. The act allows taxpayers who hold qualifying stock in small business to roll over their gains without recognizing a gain if they purchase shares in another qualifying company. It created a special alternative tax rate on unrecaptured depreciation deductions on real estate and introduced several provisions aimed at stemming the proliferation of schemes to avoid the capital gains tax.

The House had also passed a provision in 1997 that would have indexed stock and business assets for inflation starting in 2001. That provision was deleted in conference because President Clinton objected to it. The IRS Restructuring and Reform Act of 1998 shortened the holding period for long-term capital gains from eighteen months to twelve months.

Comparison with Other Countries

The taxation of realized capital gains varies greatly among developed countries. Although several tax long-term gains at lower rates than does the United States (see table 2-5), their maximum tax rates on income from other sources are higher than in the United States. Australia and the United Kingdom tax capital gains at the same rate as other income, but they allow capital gains to be indexed for inflation.[19]

Comparing federal tax rates alone may be misleading in some countries because they levy significant taxes at the local level. In Sweden, the top combined federal and local tax rate on capital gains can be as

Table 2-5. Maximum Federal Income Tax Rates, by Type of Income,
Selected Countries, 1998

Percent

Country	Long-term capital gains	Personal income	Corporate income
Australia	48.5[a]	48.5	36.0
Belgium	0	56.7	40.2
Canada	23.5[b]	31.3[c]	29.1
France	26.0[d]	58.1	41.7
Germany	0	55.9	45.0
Italy	12.5	46.0	37.0
Japan	20.0[e]	50.0	34.5
Netherlands	0	60.0	35.0
Sweden	30.0	57.0	28.0
United Kingdom	40.0[a,f]	40.0	31.0
United States	20.0	39.6	35.0

Source: American Council for Capital Formation (ACCF), "An International Comparison of Capital Gains Tax Rates," ACCF Center for Policy Research Special Report (August 1998).
a. Capital gains are indexed for inflation in Australia and the United Kingdom.
b. A lifetime capital gains exemption of Can$500,000 applies to sales of farm property or shares in certain qualified small businesses.
c. Including provincial and territorial taxes increases the top marginal rate to as high as 53 percent.
d. France allows an annual exclusion of F50,000 (about $8,315).
e. The sale of certain designated securities (including shares in corporations and convertible debentures, but excluding bonds and ordinary corporate debentures) are taxed at the lower of either a flat 20 percent rate or 1.25 percent of the sales price.
f. Shares valued at less than £6,800 (about $11,225) are exempt from capital gains tax.

high as 63 percent. (Sweden also levies a 1.5 percent annual wealth tax on families who have assets in excess of 800,000 Kroner, which is about $110,000.) In Canada, provincial taxes can raise the effective tax rate on capital gains to nearly 39 percent. Numerous special rules complicate the comparison still further.

A related question for public policy is, how do taxes affect the cost of capital for businesses? The answer depends on the whole range of taxes levied at both the corporate and individual levels and on the share of income that is subject to tax. A 1991 study by the Organization for Economic Cooperation and Development (OECD) concluded that the tax systems in about half of its member states increased the cost of corporate capital more than the system in the United States.[20] Personal taxes—including taxes on capital gains, interest, dividends, rents, and royalties—raised the cost of capital more in the United States than in most other OECD countries, but this comparison did not account for the large share of personal saving in the United States that is exempt from tax, nor for the effect of state and provincial taxes. Thus it is not clear how the United States ranks in relation to its major trading partners when all taxes are taken into account.

Two features of the tax systems of OECD countries are probably much more important than the taxation of capital gains in reducing the total tax burden on capital. First, most European countries rely more heavily on consumption taxes, such as the value added tax, than does the United States. Consumption taxes do not assess income from capital. Second, most European countries integrate the corporate tax with their individual tax systems at least in part, thereby reducing the extent to which the two tax systems create a double tax on corporate income.

Variation among the States

All forty-two states that have a broadly based income tax (including the District of Columbia) classify capital gains as taxable income, although the rates vary greatly depending on where taxpayers live.[21] Those taxes add to the overall tax burden on capital gains (and other forms of income). Because capital gains are an important component of tax bases in these states, changes in the federal tax law may substantially affect state revenues, at least in the short run, as demonstrated most strikingly by the Tax Reform Act of 1986. By stimulating a surge in capital gains in 1986, caused by taxpayers trying to avoid the tax increase, TRA86 created a windfall for states with income taxes.

In 1997 maximum income tax rates in the states ranged from 3 percent to 11 percent (see table 2-6). They added less than that amount to the overall tax burden on capital gains, because taxpayers who itemize deductions may deduct state income taxes from federal taxable income.[22] Hawaii's 10 percent rate on capital gains, for example, reduced federal tax liability by 4.0 percent (39.6 percent of 10 percent) for a taxpayer in the top tax bracket in 1997. Thus the combined

Table 2-6. Maximum Combined State and Federal Marginal Tax Rates on Capital Gains, by State, 1997[a]

Percent

| States | Maximum state tax rates | | Total combined tax rate on gains |
	Ordinary income	Capital gains	
Alabama[b]	5.0	5.0	23.6
Alaska	0	0	21.2
Arizona	5.6	7.0	25.4
Arkansas	7.0	4.9	24.1
California	9.3	9.3	26.8
Colorado	0	5.0	24.2
Connecticut	4.5	4.5	23.9
Delaware	6.9	6.9	25.4
District of Columbia	9.5	9.5	26.9
Florida	0	0	21.2
Georgia	6.0	6.0	24.8
Hawaii	10.0	10.0	27.2
Idaho	8.2	8.2	26.1
Illinois	3.0	3.0	23.0
Indiana	3.4	3.4	23.2
Iowa[b]	10.0	10.0	26.1
Kansas	7.8	7.8	25.9
Kentucky	6.0	6.0	24.8
Louisiana[b]	6.0	6.0	24.1
Maine	8.5	8.5	26.3
Maryland	5.0	3.5	23.3
Massachusetts[c]	6.0	12.0	28.4
Michigan	4.4	4.4	23.8
Minnesota	8.5	8.5	26.3
Mississippi	5.0	5.0	24.2
Missouri[b]	6.0	6.0	24.1
Montana[b]	11.0	11.0	26.7
Nebraska	7.0	7.0	25.4
Nevada	0	0	21.2
New Hampshire[d]	0	0	21.2
New Jersey	6.4	6.4	25.1
New Mexico	8.5	8.5	26.3
New York	6.9	7.0	25.4
North Carolina	7.8	7.8	25.9
North Dakota[e]	12.0	12.0	22.7

(continued)

Table 2-6. Maximum Combined State and Federal Marginal Tax Rates on Capital Gains, by State, 1997ᵃ (Continued)

Percent

| States | Maximum state tax rates | | Total combined tax rate on gains |
	Ordinary income	Capital gains	
Ohio	7.0	7.0	25.4
Oklahomaᵇ	10.0	10.0	26.1
Oregon	9.0	9.0	26.6
Pennsylvania	2.8	2.8	22.9
Rhode Islandᵉ	27.5	27.5	24.4
South Carolina	7.0	3.9	23.5
South Dakota	0	0	21.2
Tennesseeᵈ	0	0	21.2
Texas	0	0	21.2
Utahᶠ	7.0	7.0	25.4
Vermontᵉ	25.0	25.0	24.1
Virginia	5.8	5.8	24.7
Washington	0	0	21.2
West Virginia	6.5	6.5	25.1
Wisconsin	6.9	2.8	22.9
Wyoming	0	0	21.2

Sources: State individual income tax rates and capital gains tax treatment are from Federation of Tax Administrators, "State Income Taxes, 1997," available at http://sso.org/fta/ind_inc.html. Total tax rate formulas are from Bogart and Gentry, "Capital Gains Taxes and Realizations."

a. At year-end 1997, the top federal income tax rate was 39.6 percent; the top effective federal capital gains tax rate is 21.2 percent for gains on assets held more than one year. Note that the statutory federal income tax rate is used—not accounting for the phaseout of itemized deductions—to calculate the combined state and federal tax rate. An additional dollar of itemized deduction, such as state income taxes, does not usually affect the amount of itemized deductions that are reduced by the phaseout, whereas an additional dollar of income costs $.03 in lost deductions. Thus the appropriate tax rate to apply to deductions is the statutory rate.

b. State allows federal income tax to be deducted.

c. Capital gains, interest, and dividends subject to 12 percent tax rate.

d. State income tax applies only to interest and dividends.

e. State calculates tax as a function of federal tax liability.

f. One-half of federal income tax is deductible.

top federal and state tax rate on capital gains on assets held more than one year in Hawaii was 27.2 percent (the 21.2 percent federal rate, plus the 10 percent state rate, minus the deduction for state income taxes, which was worth 4.0 percent). In addition, a few states allow federal taxes to be deducted against state income tax, which reduces the effective tax rate a little more.

THE KINDS OF ASSETS
THAT PRODUCE CAPITAL GAINS

Since capital gains and losses arise when an asset changes in value, any long-lasting asset has the potential to produce a gain or loss when it is sold. The tax law, however, does not treat all increases in value as capital gains. For example, most gains on people's homes and the gains on assets held in pensions are exempt. Other assets pay out most of their income as interest, dividends, rents, or royalties and therefore do not appreciate in value much, if at all. Assets that account for the most taxable capital gains are corporate stock, businesses, mutual funds and trusts, and real estate.

Relative Importance of Capital Gains Assets

Most people do not own stocks, bonds, mutual funds, investment real estate, and businesses, in other words, the kinds of assets that generate taxable capital gains. Even so, capital gains assets represent a significant share of the total wealth held by individuals. Capital gains assets accounted for about 38 percent of the wealth of U.S. households in 1992 (see figure 3-1). Of the other assets, homes, which are most people's largest single asset, represented about 28 percent. Pensions, including tax-deferred savings plans such as individual

Figure 3-1. Composition of Assets in the Portfolios of Families, 1992ᵃ

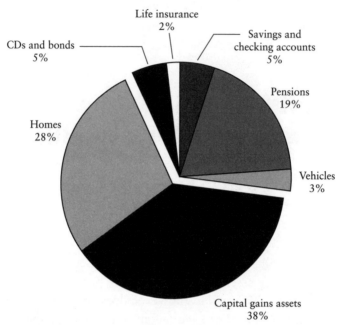

Source: Congressional Budget Office tabulations of 1992 Survey of Consumer Finance and Flow of Funds Accounts, Z.1 Statistical Release (September 1994).

a. Pension data are from the Flow of Funds Accounts. Pensions include defined contribution plans, such as individual retirement accounts, 401(k)s, and defined benefit plans.

retirement accounts (IRAs) and 401(k)s, and traditional employer-sponsored pension plans, represented 19 percent. And savings, checking, and money-market accounts, the most commonly held types of asset, accounted for only 5 percent.

If homes are included in capital gains assets, they are by far the largest component, equal to 43 percent of the total in 1992 (see figure 3-2). The most significant investment assets to produce taxable capital gains were the buildings and equipment that make up a business, which accounted for nearly a quarter of capital gains assets. Land and rental real estate made up nearly one-fifth, shares of stock in publicly traded corporations about 6 percent, and mutual funds only about 3 percent.

Figure 3-2. Composition of Capital Gains Assets, including Homes, in the Portfolios of Families, 1992

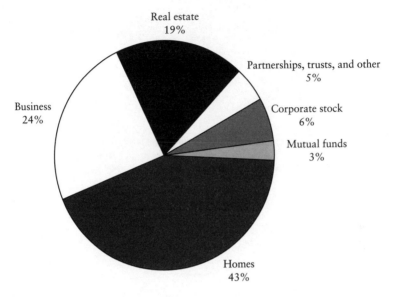

Real estate
19%

Partnerships, trusts, and other
5%

Business
24%

Corporate stock
6%

Mutual funds
3%

Homes
43%

Source: Congressional Budget Office tabulations of 1992 Survey of Consumer Finances.

For several reasons, capital gains are not distributed in proportion to capital gains assets. The exemption from tax of most home sales is one important factor. By way of example, taxable capital gains on homes constituted only about 1 percent of all gains realized in 1993 (see figure 3-3). The 1997 tax act exempted still more gains from tax. Housing capital gains would have constituted less than 0.5 percent of all gains if the new rules had been in effect in 1993.[1]

Among taxable gains, the largest category in 1993 was corporate stock, at 37 percent of the total. Mutual funds, which also consist mostly of corporate stock, contributed another 10 percent of gains. Thus nearly half of the realized gains reported that year were related to sales of stock, while business assets and real estate accounted for 15 percent and 11 percent, respectively. A little more than one-quarter of capital gains were generated by partnerships, small businesses, trusts, fiduciaries, and other assets. The assets held by partnerships

Figure 3-3. Shares of Realized Capital Gains, by Type of Assets, 1993

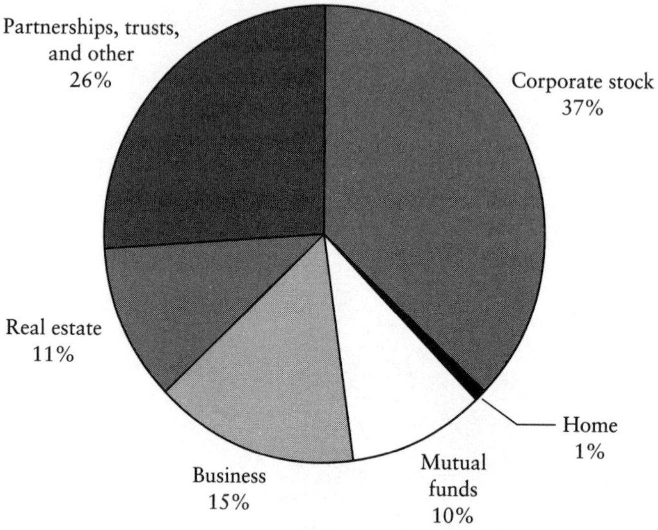

Source: Internal Revenue Service, Sales of Capital Assets, 1993.

and S-corporations are business assets, whereas those held by trusts and fiduciaries are more like mutual funds. Unfortunately, the Internal Revenue Service (IRS) combined these categories when it compiled the data on asset sales, so there is no way to untangle the components.

Assets might generate proportionately more or less capital gains for two main reasons. First, some assets—such as businesses and real estate—are relatively illiquid. Taxpayers hold onto these assets longer than more liquid assets such as corporate stock. The average stock sold in 1993 had been held for less than three years (see table 3-1), and fewer than half of stock sales qualified as long-term capital gains or losses. By contrast, residential rental property was held an average of thirteen years, business property six years, and farmland eleven years. All else equal, the assets held longer would be expected to have larger gains as a share of price.

Of course, all else is not equal, even within a single class of assets. Some assets pay out all or nearly all of their income as rents

Table 3-1. Average Holding Period, by Asset Type, 1993[a]

Number of years unless otherwise specified

Asset type	Average holding period			Number of transactions	Percent long term
	All	Long term	Short term		
Corporate stock	2.86	6.3	0.29	25,861	49
Mutual funds					
Capital gain distributions	n.a.	n.a.	n.a.	5,641	100
Sales of shares	1.44	2.06	0.5	6,738	54
Put and call options, commodities					
Futures and other securities	2.49	4.33	0.39	3,019	66
U.S. government obligations	0.55	2.48	0.2	1,321	64
State and local government					
obligations	4.34	5.32	0.47	3,026	81
Other bonds, notes, and debentures	2.81	5.74	0.27	978	78
Sale of personal residence	n.a.	n.a.	n.a.	1,966	100
Other personal residence	14.95	14.96	0.64	91	100
Residential rental property	13.25	13.46	0.34	957	97
Land other than farmland	10.66	10.81	0.57	804	99
Partnerships, S-corporations,					
fiduciaries	6.89	8.07	0.4	3,857	77
Business property	6.39	6.39	0.46	1,352	100
Livestock	3.37	3.37	0.52	616	100
Timber	40.7	40.75	0.58	79	100
Farmland	10.62	10.64	0.34	78	99
Other	6.45	9.78	0.41	3,391	82
All assets	3.59	6.74	0.3	59,775	66

Source: Leonard E. Burman and Peter Ricoy, "Capital Gains and the People Who Realize Them," *National Tax Journal*, vol. 50 (September 1997), pp. 427–51.

a. Average holding periods were weighted by sales price. Calculation excludes transactions with missing holding period information or inconsistent sales prices. Transactions totals and percent long term are based on all transactions.

n.a. Not available.

or dividends, whereas others produce little or no current income, instead accruing income in the form of capital gain. Thus the income-producing assets are likely to have relatively small gains when sold, especially in comparison with the assets that accrue income. Rates of return also vary because of differences in risk characteristics, as well as just plain luck. In sum, how much an asset appreciates in value depends on many factors.

How Assets Generate Capital Gains

Investments can generate capital gains or losses in many ways. Of course, a growing business that retains its earnings to finance expansion will accrue capital gains. If the same business chose to pay out all of its profits as dividends, however, it would produce much smaller gains or even a loss. Market conditions are also important. If demand for the goods produced by a company increases more than expected, its value increases. Another critical factor is inflation. A gold bar, say, might appreciate in value when the general price level rises, even though its intrinsic value is unchanged. Equally important are the provisions of the tax code. To take one example, an asset whose value is declining over time (because of depreciation) may generate capital gains when it is sold because the tax write-off for depreciation exceeds the true depreciation.

Growth versus Yield

Some assets accrue returns entirely in the form of capital gains. Assets in this category (called growth assets) would include trees that produce lumber (rather than fruit or nuts), because they appreciate in value as they grow without generating any cash income, and businesses in which the profits are continually reinvested, rather than paid out as dividends. The value of the growth asset arises from the expectation of future income—for example, when the tree is cut and sold—rather than from current cash income.

An asset that pays out all of its return in the form of current income (a "yield asset") is much less likely to produce a capital gain. A fruit tree is a simple example of a yield asset. Although it is a growth asset in its first few years (during which time it increases in future value but does not yield much fruit), a mature tree pays out all its returns in the form of produce, that is, current income. If the price of fruit stays the same, the value of the tree changes only because it is expected to produce less, that is, because it wears out or depreciates. For tax purposes, depreciation properly measured incurs no capital gain or loss.

A business that pays out all of its profits in the form of dividends is similar to the fruit tree. If interest rates do not change, a bond is also a yield asset. Its price will neither increase nor decrease.

Growth and yield both play a role in capital appreciation or loss. Many companies distribute some, but not all, of their profits. They pay returns in the form of both current income (dividends) and capital gains. Some investments may also generate current losses compensated for by future capital gains. Absent special rules, these losses could shelter other current income from tax. Although the current losses are eventually offset by future capital gains, those gains are taxed at lower rates. That is how the classic tax shelter worked. It was largely eradicated by the provisions of TRA86, including the full taxation of capital gains.

Market Conditions and Expectations

Investors value assets on the basis of their current and expected future earnings as compared with those available elsewhere in the market. If the earnings prospects of an asset improve, it will tend to increase in value. If those of competing investments increase, the asset will tend to decline in value. Thus stock prices fall when interest rates increase, that is, when the rate of return on bonds increases in relation to the rate of return on stocks. The price of outstanding bonds also falls when interest rates rise for the same reason.

The earnings prospects of an asset such as a business depend on profits, which are driven by supply, demand, and entrepreneurial skill. For example, a company's profits might increase because of increasing demand for its products or because of lower costs for its inputs. Profitability also depends on the efficiency with which resources are employed, which depends on the quality of management and the technologies used for production. Expectations about future profits might be affected by whether investors expect competition to increase or decrease over time, and by how investors expect management to react to future market conditions. Investors also discount assets whose returns are especially uncertain. Changes in any of these factors can result in capital gains or losses.

The Effect of Inflation

Inflation can create both capital gains and losses. By increasing the price level of assets in general, it creates capital gains even if an asset's intrinsic value is unchanged. To return to the example of the bar of gold, its real value should not change unless market conditions do. The *real* value of an asset is the value expressed in constant dollars, that is, after removing the effects of inflation. The *nominal* value is the price expressed in current dollars, that is, unadjusted for inflation. In other words, its value increases when prices go up and falls when prices drop. That is why some people invest in precious metals as a hedge against inflation. Similarly, the price of the fruit tree would go up as the price of fruit increased, and this change would generate capital gain as well as income. The price of a share of stock in a business would also increase with inflation, even if the company pays out all of its profits as dividends.

By contrast, a fixed coupon bond might decrease in value as inflation increased. An unexpected increase in inflation would increase the interest rate on new bonds, making old bonds less attractive. To provide the same yield as competing investments, the old bond must fall in value (so the fixed return becomes a larger percentage of the bond's value). Similarly, if inflation turns out to be less than expected, bonds increase in value.

More generally, inflation turns fixed income investments into assets that have capital gains and losses. The Department of the Treasury recently started selling bonds that pay returns indexed for inflation. The price of these bonds should be much less volatile in the presence of inflation than the price of Treasury bonds that are not indexed.

The Effect of Tax Provisions

Some capital gains are the result of tax rules, as in the case of the depreciation provisions for real estate. Real property is not subject to the usual rules for the recapture of depreciation deductions. When it sells for more than the depreciated basis, that excess is treated as a capital gain.[2] Thus, if the value of a building does not decline as fast as it depreciates, sales will precipitate capital gains. Moreover, with inflation, a long-held rental property is more likely to keep its value, or at least not decline as fast as it depreciates for tax purposes. Since depreciation deductions are fixed in nominal terms (unadjusted for inflation), this source of phantom capital gains increases disproportionately with the inflation rate.

Suppose a building purchased for $100,000 depreciates at a rate of 2 percent a year. The depreciation allowance under the law is 3.6 percent of its purchase price per year. (This is called 27.5-year straight-line depreciation.) If there is no inflation, this building will be worth $81,707 ($100,000 $\times$ 0.98^{10}) in ten years. But it will have taken $3,636 ($100,000 $\div$ 27.5) in depreciation for each of the ten years. Thus its adjusted basis is $63,636 ($100,000 − $3,636 $\times$ 10), or $18,071 less than its value. If sold, it would thus generate a capital gain of $18,071. If inflation in building prices was 3 percent, the property would sell for $109,808, producing a capital gain of $46,172.

The purchaser of a used asset can often restart the accelerated depreciation on the basis of the purchase price of the asset, rather than by picking up the depreciation schedule where the seller had left off. In this way, the buyer can gain additional tax benefits that can themselves contribute to the value of old assets. In an extreme case, an asset that has been fully depreciated can qualify for additional depreciation deductions if it is sold. That gives owners of assets that are subject to accelerated depreciation the incentive to sell them because they are worth more to a purchaser than they are to the current seller.

Another tax provision that could affect the value of assets would be an investment tax credit for new equipment. Such a credit would tend to reduce the value of old machinery. Capital gains tax rates themselves may affect the value of assets, as discussed in chapter 4.

HOW A CAPITAL GAINS
TAX DIFFERENTIAL AFFECTS
SAVING AND INVESTMENT

Almost everyone agrees that the rate of saving in the United States is too low. On its face, the most appealing argument for a capital gains tax preference is that it might encourage more saving, lower the cost of capital for firms, and thus spur investment and raise productivity. Many advocates of preferential treatment for capital gains would go so far as to recommend exempting all forms of saving by replacing the income tax with some kind of consumption tax. This argument makes sense if one is willing to trade off other objectives—especially fairness—for the gain in economic efficiency.

Even if one accepts the premise that a consumption tax would be a superior alternative to the current tax system, it is unclear whether taking just one step toward a consumption tax would enhance economic efficiency. The theory of second best in public finance, as mentioned in chapter 1, holds that moving part way toward an ideal tax system may actually make the economy less efficient. William Niskanen, president of the libertarian Cato Institute and an ardent proponent of tax reform, expressed the concern in the case of capital gains: "The capital gains tax cut by itself is not likely to be very helpful if you don't correct other features in the tax code. It's important to cut capital gains taxes, but only as part of the general tax reform. Cutting capital gains taxes, itself, can lead to a misallocation of capital and will be perceived as being an unfair tax cut to the rich."[1]

Making judgments in the realm of second best is a hazardous business. A qualitative assessment approaches the problem by asking the following questions:

—If the capital gains tax preference is viewed as a cut in the overall rate of tax on savings, to what extent is private saving likely to respond?

—What is the effect on the deficit—that is, on public savings—of a cut in capital gains tax rates? (This is an especially controversial question.)

—If both private and public saving are taken into account, how should a cut in capital gains taxes affect overall investment and productivity?

—When capital gains tax rates differ from the rates on other income, what is the effect on the efficiency of capital allocation?

As this and the next chapter show, such a differential between tax rates on capital gains and other income has a very small effect on the economy, and of indeterminate sign. It might increase saving, but that is not guaranteed. Although it reduces lock-in slightly, that result may not be important. In any case, there are better ways to reduce lock-in (ones that would raise revenue). It also encourages inefficient investments such as tax shelters, although this effect has been overstated. Finally, it vastly complicates the tax system. This chapter examines the direct effect of a capital gains rate differential on public and private saving and investment; chapter 5 considers the effect on the efficiency of capital allocation.

The Return on Assets

Economists measure the effect of taxes on the return from assets (known as the effective tax rate) in several ways. The simplest is to measure the difference between rates of return before and after all personal income taxes, expressed as a percentage of the before-tax return. In this way, an interest-bearing asset such as a bond subject to annual tax on the interest may be compared with an asset that pays all of its return in the form of capital gains, which are not taxed until the asset is sold. In the presence of inflation, the effective tax rate is measured in terms of the real (inflation-adjusted) rates of return (see box 4-1).

In the absence of inflation, and assuming that assets are held for only one year, effective tax rates are simple to compute and compare. The effective tax rate on a bond or other yield asset is equal to the statutory tax rate on ordinary income. Suppose that 100 shares of stock are purchased for $1,000 and produce $100 in dividends, which are subject to tax at a rate of 36 percent. The dividends generate a tax bill of $36. That would reduce the return from $100 to $64, or 36 percent. This effective rate equals the statutory rate.

If the stock paid the same $100 in the form of capital gain, the gain would be subject to the maximum tax rate on capital gains held one year, which is 20 percent. That would also be the effective tax rate. Finally, if the asset paid out part of the return as a dividend and part as capital gains, the effective tax rate would lie between the tax rate on dividends (36 percent) and the tax rate on capital gains (20 percent).

If the stock paid $25 in dividends and the capital gain was $75, the total tax would be $24 (36 percent of $25 plus 20 percent of $75). Clearly, barring any other differences between capital gains and yield assets, taxpayers would prefer to earn income in the form of capital gains, because they are subject to lower tax rates. In order to compensate, the lower tax rate on capital gains assets would require yield assets to pay higher rates of return.

This tax story is complicated by three factors: inflation, the ability to defer tax on capital gains, and the differing risk characteristics of capital gains assets and income-producing assets. In addition, capital gains and dividends on corporate stock may be taxed at the business as well as at the personal level. That double taxation further complicates the comparison between assets that pay capital gains and those that pay returns in the form of interest.

Inflation and Effective Tax Rates

Inflation makes the effective tax rate on a capital asset higher than the statutory rate. Suppose inflation is running at 4 percent and a bond paying 8 percent interest a year (the nominal return) is taxed at 28 percent on both the inflation and real returns. The tax as a share of real return will be double the tax as a share of nominal return (figure 4-1). As inflation increases, the effective tax rate does, too. At an inflation rate of 12 percent, the tax would exceed the real return, yielding an effective tax rate of more than 100 percent. In that case, the real after-tax return would be negative.

Even without a preferential tax rate on capital gains, a growth asset that pays returns in the form of capital gains, such as shares of stock in a growing business, is generally subject to a lower effective tax rate than a bond because the tax can be deferred on the asset until it is sold, rather than when income accrues. Thus, using the same statutory tax rate of 28 percent as the bond, a growth asset that is also held for ten years has a lower effective tax rate (see figure 4-1). (The holding period does not matter for the bond, because all of its income is taxed as it is earned.) The effective tax rate on the growth asset increases with inflation, but less so than the effective tax rate on the bond. The divergence grows larger as inflation increases. At a 4 percent inflation rate, the effective tax rate for the growth asset is 44 percent compared with 56 percent for the bond. At a 12 percent inflation rate, the effective tax rate for the growth asset increases by little more than half, to 70 percent; the effective tax rate for the bond doubles, to 112 percent.

A yield asset that pays all of its real return in the form of taxable dividends, such as shares of preferred stock, but that retains the inflation return (so that, all else equal, the real value of the asset is unchanged) is a hybrid between the bond, which pays out its entire nominal return, and the growth asset, which distributes nothing. Its effective tax rate lies between that of the bond and the growth asset. The benefit of deferral for the yield asset grows with the inflation rate.

At rates of inflation within recent experience in the United States, the effective tax rate can double or triple in relation to the statutory rate (and the rate that applies to wage income). Thus the theoretical argument for

BOX 4-1. Computing Effective Tax Rates

Effective tax rates measure the effect of taxes on the income earned by assets held for a long time. They provide one measure of the ways that taxes affect the incentive to save.

The effective tax rate is the percentage of reduction in the real annual return from an asset caused by taxes. If, in the absence of taxes, an asset would have earned 4 percent per year after adjusting for inflation, but taxes reduce the real return to 2 percent, then taxes reduce the rate of return by 50 percent (2 percent is 50 percent of 4 percent). In this example, the effective tax rate is 50 percent.

The effective tax rate may be computed in five steps:[1]

—Compute the nominal total return before taxes. If 100 shares of stock were bought in 1980 for $1,000, all dividends were reinvested, and the resultant holding was sold in 1990 for $2,000, the original investment would have doubled in value. That is, the total return (before considering inflation) is 100 percent.

—Compute the nominal total return after taxes. Follow the same procedure as in step 1, but include the effect of taxes on the return. Dividends are reduced by taxes before being reinvested and capital gains taxes are subtracted from the ultimate value upon sale. In the example cited in step 1, suppose taxes on dividends reduced the value of the investment in 1990 from $2,000 to $1,900, and that $100 in taxes were due on the capital gain. After taxes, the investment would yield $1,800. The total return would be 80 percent.

—Annualize the returns. That is, figure out the rate of return, which, if compounded annually, would produce the total return on an initial investment of the same amount held for the same period of time. For the previous example, $1,000 invested at 7.2 percent would be worth $2,000 after ten years. If invested at 6.1 percent, the $1,000 investment would be worth $1,800 after ten years. Thus the annualized pretax return is 7.2 percent, and the annualized after-tax return is 6.1 percent.

—Compute real annual returns. Basically, this involves subtracting the inflation rate from the annualized returns. Thus, assuming an inflation rate of 4 percent, the real pretax return is about 3 percent and the after-tax return is about 2 percent. The precise calculation is a bit more complicated because inflation and real returns compound over time. The formula for the real return is:

$$1 + \text{real return} = \frac{1 + \text{nominal annual return}}{1 + \text{inflation rate}}.$$

—For the previous example, 1 plus the real pretax return is 1.072/1.04, or 1.030.

—Compute the effective tax rate. Given these real returns, the effective tax rate is

$$\text{effective tax rate} = \frac{\text{real pretax return} - \text{real after-tax return}}{\text{real pretax return}}.$$

For the example, the effective tax rate is (0.03 − 0.02)/0.03, or 33 percent.

1. A more complete measure of effective tax rate would take into account all taxes, especially corporate income taxes. See Jane Gravelle, *The Economic Effects of Taxing Capital Income* (MIT Press, 1994).

Figure 4-1. Inflation and Effective Tax Rates on Different Types of Assets[a]

Real effective tax rate (percent)

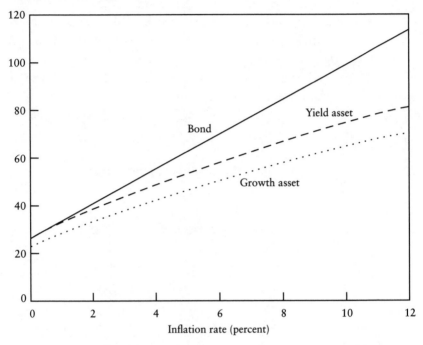

a. Assets pay a real return of 4 percent, are held for ten years, and are subject to a 28 percent tax rate.

indexing both capital income and expense appears compelling.[2] As just mentioned, however, returns paid in the form of capital gains are affected less by inflation than returns paid in the form of interest, dividends, or rent. With gains taxes at the 20 percent rate that applies to long-term gains, the differential between the bond and the growth asset is magnified further and grows with the rate of inflation.

Deferral

Deferral reduces the effective tax rate on assets that pay returns in the form of capital gains much more than on income-producing assets. Because the tax can be deferred, the money that would have gone to pay taxes can continue to earn returns until the tax is paid. A taxpayer will therefore earn a higher return by deferring tax on a growth asset than by paying tax annually on a bond if both assets have the same pretax yield. The difference in the after-tax returns is due to the tax-free compounding of interest.

Suppose that a person has $10,000 to invest either in bonds that earn 8 percent a year and are taxed on all returns every year or in shares of stock issued by a growing business that reinvests all of its profits (pays no dividends) and thus is not taxed until the stock is sold. In the first year, both the bonds and the stock earn a return of 8 percent, or $800. To simplify, assume that the investor is in the 28 percent tax bracket and that the same rate applies to capital gains (as was the case before 1997). Then the federal income tax on the interest on the bonds is $224, whereas the income tax liability on the stock is deferred until the stock is sold.

Assume that the after-tax interest on the bonds of $576 is reinvested in additional bonds, bringing the total investment to $10,576. In the second year, the bonds earn $846 in interest; the stock also earns 8 percent on its value of $10,800, or $864. The tax on interest on the bonds is $237 (28 percent of $846).[3] The tax on the stock is again deferred. At the end of the second year, the investor would have $11,185 in bonds or $11,664 in stock.

After ten years, the bonds (with the after-tax proceeds reinvested) would be worth $17,507 and the stock $21,589. If the stock was sold at this point, it would yield a taxable capital gain of $11,589. The tax, at 28 percent, would be $3,245, and the stock would have an after-tax value of $18,344, or 4.8 percent more than the bonds. The higher return from the stock is the benefit of deferring tax liability for ten years, rather than paying tax on the income as it accrues.

At the 20 percent maximum tax rate on long-term gains in effect after 1997, the tax would only be $2,318 and the after-tax value $19,271. The effective tax rate is thus much higher on the bonds than on the stock (box 4-1 explains the calculation). The annualized after-tax rate of return on the stock is 6.8 percent. (That is, $10,000 earning a 6.78 percent return compounded annually would be worth $19,271 after ten years.) At a 4 percent rate of inflation, the real after-tax rate of return is 2.7 percent. The annualized pretax rate of return is 8 percent, or a real pretax return of 4 percent. Thus taxes reduce the real return from 4 percent to 2.7 percent. The effective tax rate on the taxpayer's real income is therefore 33 percent (4 percent minus 2.7 percent divided by 4 percent). The effective tax rate in this example is higher than the 28 percent statutory rate on other income because the extra tax caused by inflation exceeds the benefits of deferral and the preferential tax rate.

Note, however, that for taxpayers in the highest brackets, the effective tax rate on gains—which would remain at 33 percent, given the assumptions—would be below the statutory rate on other income. The difference would be even larger at the recent lower rate of inflation.

In contrast, the bonds yield an after-tax return of 5.8 percent, which is the 8 percent pretax return minus the 28 percent tax. At a 4 percent rate of inflation, the real annual rate of return is 1.7 percent. The effective tax rate on the bond investment is thus 58 percent (4 percent minus 1.7 percent divided by 4 percent). The effective tax rate on bonds is higher than the effective tax rate on stock because the tax on the bonds cannot be deferred and the statutory rate is higher.

Yield assets such as shares of preferred stock represent an intermediate case. They pay out the real part of their return (again 4 percent) as a dividend and retain the inflationary part, so their inflation-adjusted value remains constant. Assuming that the after-tax dividends are reinvested, a yield asset would face a 49 percent real effective tax rate. Because only part of the tax is deferred, the effective rate on this asset lies between the rates on the growth asset and the bond.

The longer an asset is held, the more valuable deferral becomes. In the example, at a tax rate of 28 percent and a holding period of thirty years, the real effective tax rate on a growth asset falls by more than half (figure 4-2). After about twenty-five years, the benefit of deferral offsets the tax generated by inflation.

Under the 1997 tax act, capital gains tax rates decline with the holding period. That exaggerates rather than reduces the differences in effective tax rates with holding periods (figure 4-2). Although such policies might encourage investors to allocate more of their funds to longer-term investments, they cannot be rationalized as an offset to

Figure 4-2. Effective Tax Rates, by Holding Period[a]

Effective tax rate (percent)

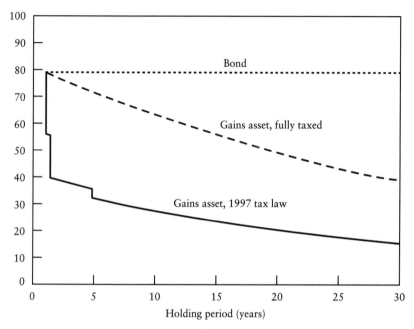

Holding period (years)

a. The gains asset accrues income at 8 percent (4 percent in real terms). The taxpayer is assumed to be in a 39.6 percent tax bracket. The capital gains tax rates are for fully phased-in TRA97.

the inflation tax. (Even the former is far from assured, as explained in chapter 8.)

The Average Tax Rate on Aggregate Capital Gains

It is sometimes useful to summarize the effect of taxes on capital gains in a single average tax rate. Economists have estimated that about one-half of capital gains are held until death or donated to charity, thus escaping tax.[4] The standard practice is to assign a tax rate of zero to those untaxed gains and infer that the average tax rate on long-term capital gains is half of the statutory rate, which is usually taken to be the top marginal tax rate on capital gains. At the current top tax rate of 20 percent, assuming that only one-half of gains are ever taxed, the average tax rate on all gains—realized or not—is 10 percent (half of 20 percent).

In addition to holding capital gains assets until death or donating them to charity, many taxpayers can reduce their tax burden by using capital losses to shelter capital gains from tax.[5] In 1994 about 12 percent of returns with a gain or loss (representing 9 percent of capital gains) had net capital losses in excess of $3,000.[6] Those taxpayers owed no *current* tax on their capital gains. Most of those with losses were not in a net loss position for long, however. For taxpayers in this situation, realizing a capital gain in the current year, even though it was untaxed currently, created a tax liability in a future year because less loss could be carried over to later years.[7] This suggests that the effective tax rate on realized long-term gains is close to the statutory tax rate.[8]

Some assets with unrealized gains face implicit taxes because avoiding the tax is costly. Taxpayers have to pay financial advisers and lawyers to arrange complicated tax-avoidance maneuvers. Even simple strategies such as borrowing to finance consumption, rather than selling an asset and realizing a capital gain, can be costly because the interest rate charged on the borrowed amount may be higher than the expected return on the marginal asset in one's portfolio. The cost of avoiding the capital gains tax is called an implicit tax. Such taxes are impossible to measure precisely, but it is safe to say that the average tax rate, including the effect of implicit taxes, is between the 10 percent rate, assuming no effect of taxes on gains held until death, and the 20 percent statutory maximum tax rate on long-term capital gains.

Saving and Investment

People save by reducing current consumption. Individuals may save by directly investing in their own businesses or by channeling their saving into stocks and bonds, bank deposits, pension funds, and the like. When a corporation reinvests its profits, it is saving on behalf of its stockholders.

Higher returns on those investments affect saving in two contradictory ways. On one hand, people are prompted to save more when the rate of return rises (economists call this the "substitution effect"). On the other hand, some may wish to save less because a higher return decreases the amount of saving needed to reach a specific future level of consumption (this is called the "income effect"). Thus some people might respond to higher rates of return by saving less. Even if they do save less, the amount of capital available to businesses may increase if people decide to take money from nonbusiness assets such as housing and invest it in financial assets, which are then made available to business.

For their part, businesses are eager to have access to such assets because they need capital to finance the array of investment projects they undertake. Some projects produce higher returns than others. The lower the cost of funds, the more projects they can profitably undertake. Thus the amount of saving demanded by the business— that is, the amount of investment it can make—increases as the return that businesses must pay falls.

Taxes drive a wedge between the amount a business earns on a new investment and the return therefrom that an individual can keep. Higher taxes on either businesses or individuals add to the size of this wedge. Businesses will not undertake new investments unless they earn a high enough rate of return before tax to cover both the taxes on the income earned by such investments and the after-tax rate of return owed to individuals. The before-tax rate of return that businesses must earn on new investments is often referred to as the cost of capital.

Taxes—including taxes on the return from saving—also affect the public surplus or deficit, and thereby national saving. Greater tax revenues or lower expenditures contribute to larger budget surpluses and thus reduce the amount of funds that the federal government must borrow. If the government borrows less, more funds are available to finance private investment. In other words, a smaller federal debt reduces the cost of capital for businesses. Thus, even though reductions in taxes on the returns from saving might stimulate private saving, they can still be counterproductive to efforts to increase total national saving if they reduce public saving.

Tax Preferences for Capital Gains

As just explained, excluding part of capital gains from taxation reduces the wedge between the return businesses earn on investments and the return individuals receive. It is also likely to reduce federal revenues and therefore increase the federal debt. If savers respond to the higher after-tax return by saving more, private saving will increase. If an exclusion increases the debt, however, public saving falls, which offsets the increase in private saving. The overall effect of cutting taxes on capital gains depends on whether the increase in private saving is greater or less than the increase in the public debt.

National Saving

A minimal test of the efficacy of an incentive for saving is that it must increase private saving by more than it costs the Treasury in lost revenue (or it must have other rationales than increasing saving). Consider a tax policy that costs the Treasury $10 billion per year and induces $5 billion in additional saving; that is, half of the "incentive" is saved and the other half consumed. National saving—the sum of private and public saving—*falls* as a result. The induced private saving is only half of what the Treasury must borrow to finance the tax incentive.

Some economists argue that this pure standard is too strict because it does not account for budget rules and politics. In their view, budget rules dictate the overall size of the budget. Hence even a minimally effective tax incentive is likely to increase national saving, because it substitutes for government spending, that is, government consumption. To take an extreme example, if a capital gains tax cut were financed by a reduction in expenditures on food stamps, national saving would probably increase because food stamps are wholly aimed at increasing consumption. Of course, if the spending reductions came in other areas, such as road building, they too might represent a reduction of public investment.

This argument may be considered an application of the theory of second best, which states that the optimal policy under given constraints (such as budget rules) may be very different from the optimal policy absent constraints. So, even though a savings incentive may do far less for national savings than a reduction in the budget, it may be the best policy available. This argument is fallacious because the political constraint is not immutable. The "second-best" argument might be a consolation to the frustrated policy adviser, but it is not an argument for advocating the inferior policy in the first place.

My analysis makes the standard economic assumption of ceteris paribus, namely that everything else is unchanged. In that context, the net effect of changing the taxation of capital gains clearly depends on its effect not only on private saving, but also on public saving.[9]

The Response of Private Saving

In fact, such a preferential tax would have little effect on the overall returns from saving. Only about 40 percent of saving produces capital gains, and most capital gains assets pay part of their return in the form of dividends, rents, and other income that would not benefit from a reduction in the tax rate on capital gains. In addition, as explained earlier, the average effective tax rate is less than the statutory tax rate.

In the case of the Taxpayer Relief Act of 1997, reducing the top rate to 20 percent increased the real after-tax return from saving by 2 to 3.5 percent, holding saving constant.[10] For taxpayers in the top tax bracket, the 20 percent rate effectively excludes slightly less than 30 percent of capital gains compared with the 28 percent rate under prior law. To put these changes in perspective, if the real after-tax rate of return is 2 percent, a 20 percent tax rate on capital gains would be expected to raise it to 2.04 to 2.07 percent on average.[11] When the burden of the capital gains tax caused by lock-in is taken into account, the effective return from saving would increase somewhat more.

If saving were highly responsive, even such a small change in the return from saving might translate into a substantial increase in private saving. Private saving might not respond at all to higher rates of return, however, because increases in the rate of return present contradictory incentives for savers, as already discussed. On the one hand, a higher rate of return increases the reward from saving and induces a substitution effect: since every dollar saved produces more future consumption, people have an incentive to substitute future consumption for current consumption (that is, save). On the other hand, the higher reward also means that a saver can achieve the same level of future consumption with less saving than would have been required at the lower rate of return. The higher rate of return makes a saver richer in the sense that current wealth levels will sustain a higher level of future consumption than before. That income effect creates an incentive to save less if current consumption is also valued. If the income effect is stronger than the substitution effect, a saver would opt for higher current and future consumption (that is, save less) in response to the higher rate of return.

Available evidence suggests that, in the aggregate, saving does not respond to the rate of return, although many would dispute that claim. Some economists even disagree about whether an increase in the rate of return would increase or decrease saving. Controversy abounds because it is difficult to measure how saving responds to changes in the rate of return, and because the predictions of theory are ambiguous. As a result, thoughtful analysts can weigh the existing evidence quite differently.

To illustrate, some argue that empirical models based on individuals' preferences for future consumption (saving) over current consumption are most consistent with economic theory and what is known about how people who account for the bulk of saving make their decisions. Estimates derived from such models suggest that saving is more responsive to the rate of return than most of the mainstream empirical economics literature suggests.[12] The more conventional approach is based on an aggregate consumption function, which measures how total consumption responds to changes in interest rates and other factors. Most of that literature finds that the response of saving is small or even negative.[13]

Another factor affecting the ways in which saving and investment respond is the extent to which businesses can absorb additional capital. If business investment were fixed, lowering the tax wedge on savings would simply increase the profits of businesses, and saving would not change at all, because savers would reap none of the rewards of the lower taxes.[14] More likely, at least over the long run, businesses would make additional investments in response to the lower cost of capital. Businesses and savers would share the benefits of the tax reduction; that is, the return from saving would increase somewhat, but not by as much as the reduction in taxes on capital gains. As a result, saving would increase by less than would be expected if one looked solely at the direct effect of the tax cut.

The discussion so far has assumed that U.S. investment is financed entirely from domestic sources. This assumption tends to exaggerate the effects of cutting capital gains taxes on U.S. investment and economic growth. If a portion of domestic investment is financed from abroad, tax incentives for saving—as distinguished from those for investment—have a limited effect on aggregate investment in the United States. Suppose a capital gains exclusion succeeds in increasing national saving, some of which flows to investment abroad, either by reducing foreign capital inflows to the United States or by motivating U.S. corporations and individuals to increase direct investment abroad. In response, the incomes of savers in the United States will probably rise, but domestic investment and output do not increase as much as saving does.

In conclusion, changes in the taxation of capital gains are likely to have little effect on private saving. Reasonable estimates of the response of saving to the rate of return suggest that private saving would increase by less than 1 percent (less than $2 billion a year). Given the uncertainty about how saving and investment react to tax incentives, the actual response might be larger or smaller (or even negative). Whatever the case, it is likely to be only a tiny fraction of total saving, because capital gains constitute a small share of the returns from saving. Moreover, the effect on the federal budget is likely to offset any response of private saving.

Public Saving

It is natural to assume that a cut in the tax rate on capital gains would reduce revenue, but it might not. Taxpayers may avoid the tax on capital gains by delaying the realization of gains, holding their assets until death, or donating them to charity. Taxpayers are even more likely to avoid realizing gains when tax rates are higher. A lower tax rate would reduce the incentive for tax avoidance and therefore could conceivably increase tax revenues. In that case, the additional proceeds would boost private saving. The available evidence suggests otherwise.

THEORETICAL EVIDENCE. The hypothesis that capital gains realizations are highly sensitive to tax rates is plausible because taxes on capital gains are easier to avoid than taxes on other sources of income, such as wages or interest. People can simply not sell assets with gains. Moreover, by borrowing, accelerating losses, deferring gains, and using options markets creatively, they might theoretically avoid capital gains taxes altogether—in the sense that an individual could achieve exactly the same stream of consumption as if there were no taxes on capital gains—assuming that capital markets were perfect and transactions incurred no costs.[15] Simpler strategies have been proposed that would yield similar results.[16] Even so, the substantial amount of annual capital gains realizations—about $260 billion in 1996—suggests that factors other than taxes play an important role in investors' decisions to sell their assets.

In view of the high level of annual asset sales, a large cut in the capital gains tax rate is unlikely to cause enough additional realizations to be self-financing. If the tax rate were cut by 50 percent, sales of assets would have to double for tax revenues to remain unchanged. That means annual sales of assets would have to equal or exceed total annual accruals of capital gains for such a response to be sustainable over the long run.[17]

Economists measure the responsiveness of capital gains to taxes using a numerical index called elasticity.[18] The greater the elasticity, the more responsive capital gains realizations are to changes in the tax rate. An elasticity of 0 would imply that taxpayer behavior is unaffected by taxes. An elasticity of 1 or greater (in absolute value) would imply that a cut in the tax rate would be self-financing: realizations would increase enough to make the additional tax revenue on the induced sales offset the direct effect of the reduction in rates.

An elasticity of less than 1 might be consistent with a positive revenue effect if taxpayers' increased realizations moved them into higher tax brackets.[19] The U.S. Congressional Budget Office examined this response and found it to be relatively small, since almost all gains were taxed at the top rate (as they are today).

To the extent that the capital gains response is actually shifting other forms of income into capital gains, a potentially more serious problem is that revenue is being lost elsewhere. Thus even an elasticity greater than 1 would not be sufficient to guarantee that revenues increase when tax rates are cut.[20]

Several models of the ways in which investors choose to sell their assets predict aggregate levels of realizations consistent with observed data.[21] These models imply that the response of capital gains realizations to tax rates—their elasticity—depends not only on how individuals value their portfolios (that is, whether the value of selling is great enough to offset the transaction cost imposed by the tax), but also on the diversity of attitudes among investors.

The models provide several insights. First, if realizations are highly sensitive to tax rates, most investors must have similar expectations about the value of their assets. They therefore choose to sell most of their assets over a narrow band of tax rates. If that were the case, there should have been few realizations of capital gains at the relatively high tax rates in effect in 1996. The question also arises, who is buying assets when everyone is selling? The models thus imply that realization elasticities much above 0.5 or 0.6 are inconsistent with observed behavior. That is, the response of capital gains to tax cuts is unlikely to be large enough for a tax cut to pay for itself.

Second, the realization response of assets with high nontax trans-action costs for selling, such as real estate, must be smaller than the response of assets with low transaction costs, such as shares of pub-licly traded stock.[22] Investors sell assets only if the expected gain is greater than the cost in terms of taxes and transaction costs. Large nontax transaction costs reduce the propensity to sell at any capital gains tax rate, which means realizations are less sensitive to tax rates. Therefore a capital gains tax preference aimed at corporate stock would probably cost less than a broader exclusion, because stock is likely to be more responsive than other assets.

EMPIRICAL EVIDENCE. A substantial body of empirical research has attempted to measure the response of capital gains realizations to tax rates.[23] Three kinds of data have been examined for this purpose: cross-sectional data, culled from thousands of tax returns filed in a single year; time-series data on total capital gains and average tax rates, collected over many years; and panel data from the tax returns of individuals over several years, which consist of both time-series and cross-sectional data. In an influential study in 1978 based on cross sections of tax returns, Martin Feldstein, Joel Slemrod, and Shlomo Yitzhaki found that capital gains are so responsive to tax changes that a rate cut would probably pay for itself. Subsequently, a number of other studies of taxpayers reached similar conclusions. But many economists have questioned these studies, arguing that the response to tax rates in a cross section of taxpayers largely reflects temporary dif-ferences in tax rates, rather than the effect of a permanent change in tax rates, such as would occur if the law changed. Feldstein, Slemrod, and Yitzhaki recognized that estimates based on cross-sectional data might overstate the effect of a rate cut. "An individual whose tax rate varies substantially from year to year," they said, "will tend to sell more when his rate is low. To the extent that low rates in 1973 are only temporarily low, our estimates will overstate the sensitivity of selling to the tax rate."[24]

In other words, cross-sectional evidence may tell a great deal about timing strategies, but little about the response to statutory changes in tax rates that are expected to be long-lasting. People often delay sell-ing assets when they face unusually high rates or accelerate realizations when their rates are unusually low. In addition, people have some ability to engineer low rates to shelter gains from tax, for example, by selling assets with losses at the same time that they sell assets with gains, or by making donations to charity.

Those problems would not be important if individuals' tax rates did not vary from year to year for reasons other than a change in tax law, or if people were not sensitive to such variations. Marginal tax rates may vary a great deal from year to year, however, so investors can benefit from carefully timing their realizations of gains (see appendix C). And taxpayers do take taxes into account in the timing of their transactions.

The response of taxpayers to the Tax Reform Act of 1986 amply demonstrates that sensitivity. The act, although passed in September of 1986, did not increase the tax rate on capital gains from the maximum of 20 percent in 1986 to a maximum of 28 percent until January 1, 1987. If taxpayers paid no attention to timing opportunities, their realizations of capital gains in 1986 would not have changed much. In fact, long-term capital gains on corporate stock in December 1986 were nearly seven times the level that they were in December 1985.[25] Clearly, taxpayers were not responding to the tax rate in 1986, which did not change, but to the change in rates expected to occur in 1987.

Another body of empirical studies looks at how total capital gains respond to changes in average tax rates over time. In this case, year-to-year variations in an individual's tax rates are averaged out in the aggregate data. Thus, with the notable exception of 1986, the aggregate capital gains tax rate has no transitory component; it represents primarily the variation in statutory tax rates.[26] Such time-series data generally suggest a much lower elasticity of response, one that would not be great enough to offset the direct revenue cost of a cut in tax rates.

Those studies suffer from the same problems that plague most time-series analysis, as well as one specific to capital gains. They have small samples (typically, fewer than forty observations), and aggregation confounds the interpretation of parameters. Perhaps most important, many unmeasured factors affecting capital gains realizations have changed at the same time as the tax rates.[27] Since 1954 the top tax rate on capital gains has changed about a dozen times, and virtually every change has been accompanied by other major tax changes, including changes in the tax rate on other income. This makes it difficult to distinguish the effect of capital gains taxes from that of the myriad other concurrent changes. As a result, time-series parameter estimates tend to be inherently unstable with respect to sample period, functional form, and choice of explanatory variables.[28]

More recent research has exploited the variation in tax rates among states to distinguish the effects of statutory variation from the year-to-year volatility in individual rates. In a sample of taxpayers, state tax rates vary in a way that is largely beyond an individual's control. The differences in behavior between similar individuals in high-tax and low-tax states provide a measure of the ways in which capital gains realizations respond to changes in statutory tax rates. (Of course, if people move to low-tax states to avoid paying tax on their capital gains, that approach also tends to overstate individuals' response to tax rates.) The additional response to their own tax status also provides a measure of the ways in which individuals respond to timing opportunities.

That empirical research resolves the mystery about why time-series estimates of realizations responses to tax rates are so small and cross-sectional estimates are quite large. Like the earlier time-series studies, the new research found the measured response to differences in state tax rates—the permanent effect—to be small and not statistically different from zero. That is, the response of individuals to permanent differences in tax rates was small or zero. By contrast, individuals' realizations of capital gains varied substantially from year to year in response to variations in their tax rates.[29] That finding is consistent with the large elasticities measured in previous studies that were based on data from cross sections.[30]

Because empirical estimates embrace a range of possible outcomes, however, they do not settle the debate about revenues. A permanent elasticity large enough for a small rate cut to be self-financing is possible, but unlikely. Even in this unlikely case, the rate cut would have to be relatively small, because the elasticity increases with tax rates in these models. In the semilog specification common in the empirical literature on realizations, the elasticity at a tax rate of 15 percent is half of the elasticity at a tax rate of 30 percent. In the extreme, the inference is obvious. No amount of behavioral feedback would cause a tax rate of zero to raise any capital gains tax revenue. And revenues from other taxes would decline, because individuals would hold fewer assets that pay income in forms other than capital gains and would try to convert wages into capital gains.

THE PRICE OF CAPITAL ASSETS. A lower tax rate on capital gains might also produce additional revenues in the short run, because it would make the assets that generate such gains more attractive to investors. The additional demand by those investors could drive up the price of capital gains assets and the higher prices would translate into greater capital gains. If the typical asset price was $100 before tax rates were cut, but $102 afterward, owners of such assets would have $2 more in capital gains when they sold them than they would have had if tax rates had not changed. Such short-run responses, of course, would be limited by market factors (see appendix D).

In the long run, the price of capital assets is determined by their replacement costs, which are unlikely to be affected by a change in the capital gains tax. Such a move does not appreciably change overall investment, just the mix of financing between equity and debt. Thus the overall demand for structures, machinery, and equipment will change little if at all, and in turn the price of business capital is unlikely to be affected substantially. As a result, over the long run, the price of capital assets is unlikely to be much different with or without a capital gains exclusion. Moreover, if investors know that the prices of assets have to return to their replacement cost over time, the short-run price increase cannot be very great. If a short-run price increase does generate capital gains, they will be at the expense of future gains. This means that any effect of higher asset prices on revenues is at best a transitory shift in the timing of collections. Overall, the effect of higher asset prices on capital gains tax revenues is likely to be small or negligible in the short run, and zero in the long run.

RECEIPTS FROM OTHER SOURCES. A differential between the tax rates on capital gains and other income creates an incentive to convert other income into capital gains, either by redirecting investments from assets that pay returns in fully taxable forms into capital gains assets, or by using tax shelters to create tax losses to offset tax liability on other income.[31] Taxpayers have an incentive to convert income into capital gains only if the taxes they avoid are greater than the additional capital gains taxes they pay. Thus at least some of the induced realizations of capital gains actually conceal a net loss in tax revenues.

Suppose all taxpayers with more than $1 million in compensation could relabel that income as capital gains at no cost. There would be a surge in capital gains realizations when the tax rate on gains fell below the rate on wages, but the additional capital gains revenues would be smaller than the lost revenues on wages. At current tax rates, for example, the lost taxes on wages would be nearly twice the additional taxes on capital gains.[32]

Although scant, the empirical evidence on the relationship between capital gains tax rates and tax receipts from other income suggests that income from interest and dividends declines when the tax differential between capital gains and other income increases.[33] This implies that an increase in the capital gains exclusion in 1983, for example, would have significantly reduced reported income from interest and dividends. Much of this evidence derives from time-series data, however, and for this and other reasons it is somewhat questionable.[34]

Overall Effect of a Capital Gains Tax Cut

As the foregoing discussion makes clear, a cut in the tax rate on capital gains is unlikely to have much effect on saving and investment because saving is relatively unresponsive to tax incentives, capital gains are a small part of the overall return from saving, and businesses require lower costs of capital in order to use the additional savings that are generated. Moreover, although taxpayers respond to a lower tax rate in a way that reduces the cost in terms of reduced revenue, there is still a relatively large revenue cost for cutting tax rates on capital gains.

As an example of the likely magnitude of effects, suppose that in 1997 the government had enacted a 50 percent exclusion in place of

Table 4-1. Change in Saving and Investment Caused by a
50 Percent Capital Gains Exclusion under Different Assumptions[a]

Percent

| Assumption | Assumed elasticity of supply of saving[b] | | | | | | | |
| | Five-year period | | | | Ten-year period | | | |
	0	0.2	0.4	0.6	0	0.2	0.4	0.6
No budget effect								
Change in saving								
(billions of dollars)	0	9.6	16.5	21.7	0	22.8	39.0	51.2
Percent change	0	0.6	1.0	1.3	0	0.6	1.0	1.3
Joint Committee on Taxation estimated budget effect[c]								
Change in savings								
(billions of dollars)	−14.3	−2.3	6.3	12.8	−63.6	−30.2	−6.4	11.4
Percent change	−0.9	−0.1	0.4	0.8	−1.6	−0.8	−0.2	0.3

Source: Congressional Budget Office.

a. Estimates assume that the 50 percent exclusion would reduce the cost of capital by 3.5 percent and that the elasticity of investment demand is −1.0. See appendix A.

b. The elasticity of supply of saving is an index of how saving responds to higher rates of return.

c. The budget effect is the revenue loss estimated by the Joint Committee on Taxation.

the 28 percent maximum rate. This scenario will better show how capital gains taxes affect saving and investment than what was actually done because it does not include the effects of timing gimmicks, such as the mark-to-market option in 2001, and special rates for certain classes of assets such as real estate and small businesses. A 50 percent exclusion would have reduced the maximum tax rate on capital gains to 19.8 percent—half of the maximum statutory rate on other income—which is about equal to the 20 percent maximum rate actually enacted. If the reduction in the cost of capital is at the top of its range (3.5 percent), investment is moderately responsive to the cost of capital, and the saving elasticity is at about the midpoint of its empirical range (typically thought to be between 0.0 and 0.4), personal saving would increase by 0.6 percent, or about $10 billion over five years (see table 4-1).

A 50 percent exclusion would have reduced tax revenues by about $14 billion over five years, according to the Joint Committee on Taxation.[35] As a result, the net effect of the exclusion on both public and private saving would be a slight reduction: about $2 billion over five years, or less than 0.1 percent of personal saving (for the methodology underlying these estimates, see appendix B). Over a ten-year period, saving would fall by more: about $30 billion, or 0.8 percent of personal saving. The decline in saving grows because the revenue cost is more than three times larger in the second five years than in the first five years. The effect on the first five years includes a short-term spurt of realizations soon after the exclusion is put in place (an "unlocking" of gains) that would not be sustained.

Larger or smaller responses of saving are possible, given the uncertainty about how people and businesses respond to tax changes. As discussed earlier, some empirical evidence suggests that saving does not respond at all to tax changes; that is, the saving elasticity is zero. In that case, personal saving would be unchanged by an exclusion, but the lost tax revenues would add to the debt. In the short run (five years), public saving would fall by about $14 billion; over ten years, it would fall by $64 billion. The saving elasticity could also be larger. At an elasticity of 0.4, personal saving would increase by 1 percent, enough to offset the revenue cost over five years, but not over ten years. At an elasticity of 0.6—the largest estimate consistent with mainstream empirical research—saving would increase by enough to offset the lost tax revenues over both the five and ten-year intervals. During the first five-year period, the increase in personal saving more than offsets the revenue loss, increasing public and private saving by about $13 billion. Over ten years, the induced saving falls slightly, to about $11 billion. Thus even if a very optimistic saving response is assumed, a cut in the capital gains tax is unlikely to increase national saving over the long run.

Of course, the unpredictability in the other parameters, including the uncertainty about how revenues respond to tax rates, might mean that a cut in capital gains tax rates would increase saving, but the literature suggests that such a response is unlikely. Whether saving increases or decreases as a result of such a cut, the change is likely to be small compared with total saving and the size of the economy.

HOW A TAX PREFERENCE
AFFECTS THE EFFICIENCY OF
CAPITAL ALLOCATION

The preceding analysis suggests that a tax preference for capital gains is unlikely to have much effect on the level of net national saving. However, a lower tax rate on capital gains might still be beneficial if it caused capital to be allocated to more productive uses. Proponents argue that lower rates encourage risk-taking and entrepreneurship, reduce lock-in, and partly offset the double taxation of corporate income. Critics counter that they are more likely to lead to unproductive tax shelter investments and other schemes to avoid or evade the higher tax rates on ordinary income.

Some analysts believe that not enough capital is available to fund new ventures and high-risk investments. A lower tax rate on capital gains might increase the amount of capital available for these uses because it would raise the after-tax return on risky investments that pay returns in the form of capital gains. But it would also reduce the value of the deductions created by those investments when they fail; the two effects counteract each other somewhat. The majority of capital in formal venture capital markets is supplied by corporations, institutions such as pension funds, and foreign investors, none of which are directly affected by the tax on individuals' capital gains. Investment in new firms, however, which rely more heavily on informal sources of capital from family and friends, might be more sensitive to income tax rates on capital gains.

Sometimes, individuals are deterred from selling appreciated assets by the prospect of taxes on the capital gains. A lower tax rate reduces the cost of selling assets that they believe are less profitable than alternative investments. Reducing lock-in has little effect on large, established, capital markets, however, because so many of the assets there are held by investors who are unaffected by the individual income tax. But reducing lock-in is helpful to people who own only one asset that has a large capital gain, such as a farm or business. The lower tax rate would facilitate the selling of a business and the investment of the proceeds elsewhere.

In the U.S. tax system, taxing capital gains and dividends earned by individuals from holdings of corporate stock corresponds to a second round of taxation, because the corporate income tax already taxes their earned income. A lower tax rate on capital gains reduces that double taxation and therefore may encourage individuals to invest in corporate stock.

Although a larger differential between the tax rates on capital gains and other income might encourage productive investment through the channels just discussed, it would also encourage unproductive investment in the form of tax shelters. In the classic tax shelter, investors take advantage of such a difference to create artificial losses. If the interest expense is fully deductible, but capital gains taxed at only half the rate of ordinary income, a dollar of interest expense that produces $1 of capital gain reduces the investor's taxable income by 50¢. Deferral makes such an investment even more profitable, because the interest deductions may be taken for many years before the capital gain is realized and subject to tax. Many tax shelters in the early 1980s took advantage of tax deferral and the difference between the tax rates that applied to capital gains and those that applied to deductions of interest and depreciation. Those tax benefits made many unproductive investments profitable, but society's scarce capital would have been better spent on other investments that were not so favored by taxes. Moreover, tax sheltering reduces tax receipts, compounding the budgetary cost of capital gains tax preferences.

The tax law contains many provisions aimed at discouraging tax shelters, which add to the complexity of the tax system. Such rules might be simplified or, in some cases, even dispensed with, if the rate differential were removed.

Thus it is unlikely that the benefits of low taxes on capital gains are equal to their costs. Creating a tax system that has lower taxes on capital without creating new inefficiencies would require fundamental tax reform, as discussed in chapter 8.

Lock-In

The lock-in effect provides a powerful incentive to hold assets with large accumulated gains, even if other assets would be more productive. In thinly capitalized markets, lock-in can trap capital in inefficient investments that might be used more productively elsewhere. The argument is clearly most relevant in the case of a small privately held business, the proprietor of which might keep it going long after it should have been shut down. It is less relevant in the stock market. Even if taxable individuals are reluctant to sell shares of companies they expect to perform poorly, pension funds (which hold about half of all stocks) and foreign investors are unaffected by the capital gains tax. They would quickly sell their shares until the price reflected the prospects of the company. As a result, the lock-in of individual investors should have little or no long-run effect on asset values, although it might affect the speed of adjustment in the market.

The lock-in effect can still be costly to individuals. They may find that the tax cost of realizing capital gains prevents them from diversifying or rebalancing their portfolios. That inefficient level of risk-bearing is part of the excess burden of the capital gains tax. This burden might be large enough to make a cut in the capital gains tax beneficial, even though it might reduce net national savings, depending on how sensitive realizations and corporate dividend payouts are to the tax rate on capital gains.[1]

A tax on capital gains might also have a reverse lock-in effect, causing taxpayers to hold long-lived assets, such as trees, either too long or not long enough.[2] The tax may cause an investor to harvest earlier than he would in the absence of taxes, because at the same time that the tax on accrued gains rewards deferral, future gains are subject to tax. Thus the after-tax value of the asset may not appreciate in value fast enough to compete with an alternative investment, such as a new tree. From a social perspective, whether the investor sells too soon or too late depends on the tax compared with the benefit of deferral and the opportunity cost of the resources used to produce the asset, such as land.

Yet another kind of lock-in effect that might occur is actually intensified by the differential between the tax rate on capital gains and other income. It would give corporate managers an incentive to retain earnings rather than pay them out in the form of dividends. Here, lock-in allows corporate managers to retain earnings even if internal investments earn below-market rates of return. Researchers have calculated that a capital gains tax cut could make society worse off on balance if realizations are not very sensitive to taxes but dividends are responsive to their tax price.[3] The loss to society results from the combination of lost tax revenues and the increased corporate lock-in effect, which more than offsets the gain for individuals from reduced lock-in. Some believe the loss to society is likely to be small, however, because corporations have the same investment opportunities as individual investors. Thus if corporate managers act in the interest of shareholders, retained earnings will earn a competitive rate of return.

All of this research assumes that individuals own a single asset. That is the worst case for lock-in. In fact, the people who realize most of the capital gains own many assets (see chapter 6). If investors are well diversified, lock-in is a less severe problem. For one thing, a large portfolio almost surely contains assets with both gains and losses, and an investor can sell the assets with losses to shelter some or all of the gains from tax.[4] For another, an investor with a large portfolio can purchase assets to divest much or all of the risk associated with a particular investment. The simplest way to do this is to sell a portfolio asset short; this kind of transaction, called "short against the box," was thwarted by the Taxpayer Relief Act of 1997 in the wake of some highly publicized abuses involving this technique. Nevertheless, other less egregious methods will always be legal.[5] For example, taxpayers can reduce the risk associated with lock-in on a particular asset by purchasing other assets whose returns are negatively correlated with those on the locked-in asset.

Some analysts have questioned whether individual trading is based on information (knowledge about future prospects for assets) or "noise" (ignorant speculation). If individuals are primarily noise traders, market efficiency is not enhanced by trading.[6] In addition, there is some evidence that investors may overreact to short-term information such as firms' reports of earnings and profits, while discounting long-term prospects of firms.[7] Trading based on "short-termism" may cause asset prices to systematically deviate from the inherent value of firms. Noise trading can increase the variability of market prices and make it harder for expert traders and arbitrageurs to extract information about the true value of investments. Such trading carries an additional social cost because of the transaction costs involved in nonoptimal trading. Thus lock-in might actually be socially desirable.

On balance, the consequences to efficiency of the additional trading induced by reductions in capital gains taxes are unlikely to be significant, although the evidence on market efficiency is decidedly mixed. Some researchers conclude that one cannot reject the hypothesis of efficient markets.[8] But the benefits to individuals of diversifying their portfolios is unlikely to be great. Individuals with large portfolios who trade often account for a large share of realizations of capital gains (as demonstrated in chapter 6). Those individuals have considerable control over portfolio risk, even if some of their assets are "locked in" because of capital gains taxes. They can diversify by trading in options or purchasing securities whose returns are negatively correlated with the returns of the assets in which they are overinvested. The gain in efficiency to these individuals of unlocking old assets stems not from lower portfolio risk, but rather from the savings of transaction costs that they would otherwise incur in trying to minimize their risk through these alternative means.

Lock-in is a serious problem only for taxpayers who own one or a few capital gains assets—for example, a family business—and who cannot diversify the returns on those assets. Those people account for a very small share of capital gains.

Finally, it should be noted that a primary cause of the lock-in effect is the failure to tax capital gains at death. Were capital gains taxed at death, taxpayers could defer but not avoid entirely tax liability on capital gains. This would significantly reduce the tax incentive to hold onto assets. If lock-in is an important issue, policymakers should consider changing the tax treatment of capital gains at death. Taxing capital gains at death would have the added benefit of raising about $9 billion a year at current tax rates, and more if taxes on capital gains were increased.[9]

Risk-Taking

Because capital gains often arise from risky investments, some argue that taxing them discourages risk-taking. Like everything else in this debate, the issue is not that simple. A tax on capital gains lowers the after-tax return from investing in risky assets. By itself that would discourage risk-taking. As long as capital losses are also deductible, however, the tax decreases the variability of returns, which makes risky assets more attractive.[10] On balance, fully taxing capital gains may have little effect on investors' decisions to assume risk.

Of course, some would argue that the tax system should not be merely neutral with respect to risk, but that risk-taking and entrepreneurship should be encouraged. The evidence in the economics literature is mixed on this point. According to economist Agnar Sandmo, who conducted a survey of the literature, "It seems reasonable to conclude that the few studies which have been made of the optimum taxation of risky assets cannot provide any *a priori* foundation for a recommendation that risky assets be taxed at higher or lower rates than safe ones."[11]

To illustrate these conflicting effects, suppose an investor has to decide whether to invest $1,000 in a project that pays $3,000 and $0 with equal probability. Absent taxes, the possible outcomes are a gain of $2,000 and a loss of $1,000, with an expected (mean) return of

$500 (the average of +$2,000 and –$1,000). At a tax rate of 40 percent, the gain would be reduced to $1,200, but the loss would also be reduced to $600. Similarly, the expected return falls to $300. Although the expected gain is reduced by 40 percent, the maximum loss is also reduced. In essence, the government is sharing in the risk of the investment in exchange for a hefty insurance premium. Taxation in this example is equivalent to an insurance policy with a premium of $800, which pays $1,200 in the case of a loss and $0 otherwise.

Now consider the effect of cutting the tax rate in half, to 20 percent. In this case, the possible outcomes are a gain of $1,600 or a loss of $800, with an expected return of $400. Taxation at the lower rate is equivalent to half the insurance: for a "premium" of $400, the government will pay $600 in the case of a loss and $0 otherwise. Some investors would prefer more insurance than this (a higher tax rate) and some less (a lower rate). Clearly, the insurance component is most attractive to those who are most averse to risk. That is, taxation of capital gains encourages risk-taking by those who would be least likely to undertake it in the absence of taxes.[12]

In fact, as explained earlier, the law provides further inducements to risk-taking by allowing taxpayers to defer the taxation of gains but to claim losses when they occur. In effect, the "full" taxation of capital gains amounts to full deductibility for losses with only partial taxation of gains. Using the rule of thumb that only half of gains are effectively taxed, whereas losses are fully deductible, taxes would not change the expected return at all in the previous example but would reduce the variance of returns. If taxed at the 40 percent statutory tax rate, the government would take $400 if the investment succeeded and pay $400 if it failed. This is in effect insurance on actuarially fair terms, which any risk-averse investor would choose to purchase. In this case, taxation surely encourages risk-taking.[13]

Of course, if losses cannot be fully deducted, taxing gains could penalize risk-taking by similar logic. (Ignoring the benefits of deferral and the nontaxation of gains at death, the government would be taxing gains in full, but subsidizing losses only in part.) The tax law does include limits on the deductibility of capital losses. While capital losses are fully deductible against capital gains, only $3,000 of capital losses in excess of capital gains may be deducted against ordinary income in a year. Excess losses must be carried over to later years. In theory, a taxpayer may have a large loss that can only be deducted over the course of many years.

In fact, between 1987 and 1994, 72 percent of taxpayers with losses were not subject to the loss limit because their losses were small or they had other gains.[14] Among those with net losses in excess of the limit, two-thirds were able to fully deduct their losses against gains or other income within two years, and more than 90 percent were able to do it within six years. Even that calculation overstates the effect of the loss limit, because some taxpayers were deliberately realizing losses and deferring gains to reduce their capital gains tax liability.[15] However, that picture may be skewed by the fact that taxpayers who wish to realize gains have a stronger incentive to realize losses at the same time in comparison with taxpayers without gains. Nonetheless, the available evidence suggests that the limitation on capital losses is not particularly onerous for most taxpayers.

Some analysts raise the possibility that the capital gains loss limit deters lower-income people from investing in their own businesses. Since their business represents their only capital gains asset, these individuals cannot deduct possible losses against other gains, and thus the loss limit is likely to be binding. Evidence suggests that this is not the case. In fact, the $3,000 loss limit is relatively large compared with the size of loss that most lower-income investors incur. Investors in the lowest tax bracket are the least likely to have a net capital loss in excess of $3,000. When they have such a loss, they spend the fewest years in that situation.[16]

With full deductibility of capital losses, the first-order effect of a reduction in the tax rate on capital gains is to encourage more investments in assets that produce capital gains but have little or no risk. For these assets, the lower tax rate raises the expected after-tax return, with little effect on the riskiness of the investment, since it has low variance. The lower rate may also encourage more people to invest in assets that pay returns in the form of capital gains, which are probably inherently riskier than other kinds of assets, but the overall effect on risk-taking is, at best, ambiguous. On balance, a capital gains tax preference is likely to have little effect on risk-taking and might even encourage it.

Entrepreneurship

As just mentioned, a primary drawback of the current tax treatment of capital gains is that the limitation on capital losses may discourage investment in small businesses. Some see a reduction in the tax rate as an effective way to stimulate the supply of venture capital, which is a source of equity for risky ventures, often in high-technology areas. Others remain skeptical that tax cuts act as incentives for entrepreneurship.[17] Indeed, there is no empirical evidence that lower taxes would do so.

Although individual investors provide virtually all of the human capital invested in new ventures—that is, the education, experience, and special skills—they contribute only a small fraction of the financial capital. Economist James Poterba found that "more than three-quarters of the funds that are invested in start-up firms are provided by investors *who are not subject to the individual capital gains tax,* such as institutional investors, foreigners, and corporations."[18] Therefore changes in the individual capital gains tax rate may have only minimal effects on the supply of capital for new ventures.

People in the venture capital industry counter that much of the funding for the earliest stages of new ventures comes from the entrepreneur's family and friends, who are subject to capital gains taxes. Because that funding is outside the formal venture capital markets, data for estimating the importance of taxes in those decisions are not available. For investors in this group who may not be able to diversify to reduce their risk, a lower capital gains tax rate might make a big difference.

But current tax law also provides benefits for small entrepreneurs. Investors in stock in small businesses issued as part of an initial public offering are able to exclude up to 50 percent of the capital gain, and the included portion of the gain is taxed at a maximum rate of 28 percent. The law also allows businesses to deduct fully (expense) the first $17,000 of investment.

Moreover, a large part of what entrepreneurs bring to a new business is their human capital: they take low salaries in the initial phase of a business in exchange for the prospect of capital gains in the future. Since the entrepreneurs do not pay tax on the wages that they invest (by taking a lower salary than they could earn elsewhere), they implicitly receive a current tax deduction for this contribution. If the investment succeeds, the entrepreneur may earn a large capital gain, but unlike the outside investor who contributes after-tax earnings to the enterprise, the entrepreneur contributed before-tax earnings. As a result, the human capital investment is subject to one level of taxation, whereas the outside investor is subject to two. In other words, the entrepreneur's investment of human capital is treated the same as other tax-favored investments, such as individual retirement accounts and pensions.

Double Taxation of Corporate Equity

Some analysts advocate expanding the tax preference for capital gains in order to offset the double taxation of corporate income. The corporate income tax, which applies only to dividends and retained earnings, distorts the allocation of capital between the corporate and non-corporate sectors and encourages inefficiently high levels of debt in the corporate sector. The ideal solution to this double taxation would be to integrate the corporate income tax. Corporate income, whether or not it is distributed as dividends, could be treated as income earned by shareholders and then taxed only at the individual level. Such a system would remove the bias both against corporate equity in general and against corporate distributions in particular, since shareholders' tax liabilities would be unaffected by corporate dividend policies. If this ideal tax encouraged dividend payouts, it would remove a possible source of inefficient investment at the corporate level.

If such integration proved unfeasible, a second-best measure might be to permit a tax preference specifically for capital gains on corporate stock.[19] This would reduce the cost of equity financing for corporations and thus reduce the incentive of corporations to take on too much debt. In theory, indexing capital gains on corporate stock could eliminate the effect of inflation on the user cost of corporate capital.[20] As discussed earlier in the chapter, however, a preferential rate on capital gains on stock discourages corporations from paying out earnings in the form of dividends.

These arguments do not justify an across-the-board preference for capital gains. If the purpose of the tax preference is to offset the tilt in tax burden in favor of noncorporate assets, providing a tax benefit to both corporate and noncorporate assets is counterproductive. Except to the extent that corporate stock pays a greater proportion of its returns in the form of capital gain, an across-the-board cut would not make investors more prone to invest in corporate stock than other capital gains assets.

Moreover, granting the tax subsidy to both noncorporate and corporate assets raises the cost-benefit ratio in two ways. First, it roughly doubles the static cost of the tax subsidy; as noted in chapter 3, about half of capital gains arise from corporate stock and mutual funds. Second, as explained in chapter 4, realizations of corporate stock are likely to be the most sensitive to tax rates. Although the induced realizations from cutting taxes on corporate stock alone might be large enough to be self-financing, the induced realizations on illiquid assets such as land and real estate are much smaller. In consequence, the estimated revenue loss associated with an across-the-board tax cut would be more than twice the revenue loss from a targeted tax cut for corporate stock.

Tax Shelters

One thing is certain about a tax preference for capital gains: it creates a strong incentive to make investments that pay returns in the form of capital gains, whether they are economically efficient or not. A preference for capital gains, combined with generous depreciation schedules and recapture rules, made investments in "see-through office buildings"—that is, office buildings with few tenants—seem profitable in the early 1980s. By encouraging such inefficient investments, the preference might actually retard economic growth.

Deferral is a key element of tax shelters, which were severely curtailed as a result of several provisions of Tax Reform Act of 1986, including the full taxation of capital gains. The ideal tax shelter investment generates little capital income but appreciates over time. Suppose that an investment of $100,000 produces no income but appreciates in value at a rate of 8 percent a year. If the investor could borrow at a rate of 10 percent, this investment would generate a loss of $2,000 a year before taxes (the 8 percent appreciation less the 10 percent interest expense). Obviously, the investment should not be undertaken. But if interest is fully deductible and capital gains are only partly taxed, this investment might become profitable. If ordinary income is taxed at 40 percent and capital gains at 20 percent, even if the investment were held for only one year, the taxpayer would make money on this unproductive investment. Deduction of the interest would be worth $4,000 ($10,000 in interest, deducted at a 40 percent rate). But the capital gain of $8,000 would cost the taxpayer only $1,600 in taxes. Thus the $2,400 in tax savings would more than offset the $2,000 pretax loss on the investment. If the taxpayer held the investment longer, he or she would save even more in taxes, because the interest expenses would be deducted every year, whereas the ultimate tax liability could be deferred for many years. The investment is a tax shelter because it creates current interest deductions to shelter other income from tax, and it is profitable only because of taxes.

An even better tax shelter allows the investor to take depreciation deductions that exceed the rate at which the investment declines in value. Those depreciation deductions are also deductible at the tax rates that apply to ordinary income, sheltering even more current income from tax. On real estate investments, such deductions are ultimately taxed as capital gains at a lower rate, generating more tax profits for investors in the same way that interest deductions do.[21] For other investments, the excess depreciation deductions are "recaptured"—that is, they are taxed as ordinary income when the investment is sold—but the taxpayer benefits because he or she receives an interest-free loan from the government equal to the value of the excess depreciation deductions.

A capital gains tax preference may create an incentive to "churn" depreciable assets, that is, to sell assets solely for tax purposes. Before

TRA86 was passed, investors in real estate and certain other long-lived assets had an incentive to sell the assets after a relatively short period to other investors who could take full advantage of the interest arbitrage described above as well as accelerated depreciation deductions. A 1987 Treasury Department study found that, under reasonable assumptions, churning of residential rental real estate could have been virtually eliminated by the repeal of the partial exclusion of capital gains alone, even if the other reforms enacted in 1986 had not taken place.[22]

Tax sheltering is problematic for two reasons. First, it is inefficient. Resources spent avoiding tax are wasted; they could otherwise be invested in productive activities. Second, tax shelters by their very nature are designed to reduce tax liability. Though this revenue loss could exceed any gain due to induced realizations (see chapter 4), it is not measured in the studies of how realizations respond to capital gains tax rates.

The tax-sheltering response to a large capital gains tax differential today is likely to be different from what it was before TRA86. At the same time that Congress repealed the partial exclusion on capital gains, it enacted other provisions aimed in part at curtailing tax shelters. The passive loss limitation, for example, restricts the ability of investors to deduct tax-shelter losses. In general, taxpayers may not deduct losses on passive investments—that is, losses on businesses that the taxpayer does not actually participate in managing—against other income. The losses may be carried over and used to offset future income from the investment, including capital gains, but offsetting capital gains with passive losses eliminates the benefit of lower rates on capital gains. Similarly, the investment interest limitation constrains the ability of investors to deduct interest expense incurred to finance investments to the extent of investment income. These provisions, as well as longer depreciation lives for durable assets—also enacted in 1986—make traditional tax shelters less attractive.

Innovations in financial markets now threaten to stimulate much more tax-sheltering activity than ever occurred before the 1986 act. Harvard law professor Daniel Halperin makes the case as follows: "We have had little experience with the confluence of capital gain relief and the widespread use of derivatives. It seems possible that investors will seek to use financial products to convert nearly all income to long-term capital gain."[23] That is, the kinds of tax-avoidance strategies once envisioned only in theory have become practical possibilities, stimulated by the advent of highly developed financial markets, increasingly sophisticated financial advisers, and a large tax incentive for developing these alternatives.[24]

Some of these tax-sheltering schemes were profitable when the top tax rate on capital gains was 28 percent. But total income tax receipts have soared, so it is not quite time to declare that the sky is falling. The risk, however, is that, prodded by the large differential between ordinary income and capital gains tax rates, financial advisers will develop highly efficient means of converting ordinary income into capital gains, ones that can be implemented by a computer program with little or no human interaction. If that occurs, the genie will have been let out of the bottle. Reducing or eliminating the differential between capital gains and other income may not reverse the erosion of the tax base.

Costs of Administering and Complying with the Income Tax

A capital gains preference conflicts with the widely supported objective of tax simplification. Complicated recapture rules and rules on original-issue discount obligations, installment sales, limitations on the deductibility of passive losses and interest expense, and so on become necessary to curtail tax shelters and other kinds of unproductive activities. Such limitations make the system harder and more costly to comply with and more expensive to administer. Moreover, because a larger differential in tax rates increases the rewards for cheating—that is, mischaracterizing fully taxable income (such as wages or interest) as capital gains—it would require more enforcement effort by the Internal Revenue Service. A lower rate on capital gains does, however, increase the incentive to report capital gains. Thus it might deter abuse on that margin. If taxpayers are successful at sheltering their income from tax, the rates on other income must be higher. Higher tax rates intensify the inefficiency of the income tax and raise concerns about its fairness.

Overall Effect on the Economy

Low tax rates on capital gains, some say, could have miraculous effects on the economy. Allen Sinai predicted in congressional testimony in 1997 that a 50 percent cut in rates from their 1996 levels (along with a smaller cut in the tax rates paid by corporations) would increase the capital stock by $76 billion (1.1 percent) in just five years. The gross domestic product (GDP) would increase by $67 billion (0.8 percent). In just two years, half a million jobs would be created, and the personal saving rate would increase by 0.7 percentage points in the first year![25]

These claims are so extreme that they should be observable in the data. On the contrary, economic growth has shown no perceptible effect even though capital gains tax rates have changed a dozen times in the past forty-five years (figure 5-1). From 1954 to 1996, the correlation between the percentage change in real gross domestic product and the maximum tax rate on capital gains is essentially zero (−0.01). Any effect of the changes probably occurs with a lag, but lagged capital gains tax rates are not significantly related to the rate of growth of GDP either.[26] Furthermore, no more sophisticated study has established any impact of capital gains on economic growth.

Rather, any effects of capital gains taxes on the economy are relatively subtle, which is good news. On balance, a large across-the-board tax preference for capital gains—as now exists—probably depresses the economy slightly. It is likely to have no effect on and may even retard saving and investment. It provides a small benefit by offsetting the lock-in effect (something that could be accomplished more effectively by taxing capital gains at death).

But a large tax preference for capital gains entails costs. To reiterate, it creates opportunities for tax shelters, inefficient tax avoidance, and evasion. A large differential between the effective tax rates on capital

Figure 5-1. Capital Gains Tax Rates and Economic Growth, 1954–95

Percentage change
in real GDP (solid)

Maximum marginal tax rate
on gains (dashed)

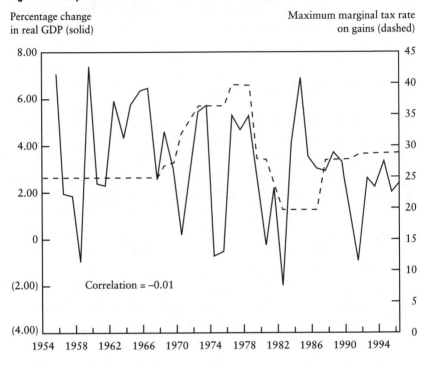

income earned in the form of capital gains and the rates on expenses such as interest and depreciation can make economically inefficient projects profitable after tax. Such tax shelters waste society's scarce resources. A large differential between the tax rates on ordinary income and those on capital gains encourages people to devise schemes to convert ordinary income into capital gains, for example, by converting wages into qualified stock options. It also provides a financial incentive to cheat. By making the definition of income much more important to the determination of tax liability, a differential also makes the income tax vastly more complex and more costly to enforce.

As pointed out in chapter 4, the supply-side claim that cutting taxes would increase tax revenues remains unsubstantiated. The best econometric evidence shows that the timing of capital gains is extremely sensitive to year-to-year fluctuations in tax rates, but that the realization of those gains is little affected by changes in statutory tax rates of long duration. As a result, cuts in tax rates almost surely depress taxes paid on capital gains. Another problem with this argument is that it fails to take into account the indirect effect of lower capital gains tax rates, which is to reduce tax collections from other sources. Innovations in financial markets may cause the revenue loss from conversion of other income into capital gains to become even larger in the future. Without a strong economic argument for a capital gains tax preference, the issue comes down to one of fairness, as discussed in chapter 6.

6

WHO HAS CAPITAL GAINS?

A fundamental objective of tax policy is to tax people in similar circumstances the same way. The taxation of capital gains when realized, rather than as they accrue, makes it difficult to achieve that objective. One problem is that the capital gains people realize are not the same as the income they earn from the appreciation of capital assets. Someone who sells a family business or home may realize a capital gain that far exceeds the income he or she earned in that year. In other years, the same person may have earned capital gains that were not reflected in income because they were unrealized. An investor with a large portfolio of assets who engages in aggressive tax planning might appear to have little or no capital gains, despite substantial appreciation in the value of the portfolio. Inflation further complicates such comparisons, because two people with the same nominal gain could have very different real gains after adjusting for inflation, and inflation can cause capital income—including capital gains, interest, and dividends—to be overstated when compared with other forms of income, such as wages.

Because it is difficult to tax capital gains in the same way as other forms of income, people who own assets that produce capital gains can end up being taxed more heavily or less heavily than other taxpayers. To try to determine who is affected by such disparities and by changes in the tax treatment of capital gains, this chapter examines data on the ownership of capital gains assets and the realization of capital gains from three sources: the Federal Reserve Board's 1992 Survey of Consumer Finances (on wealth holding), 1993 income tax returns, and a panel of returns for taxpayers over a ten-year period (1979–88).

The data paint a very complex picture of who owns capital gains assets and who sells them. A surprisingly large fraction of taxpayers own capital assets and are thus potentially subject to tax on capital gains. About half of the families in the United States own assets such as stocks, bonds, real estate, and businesses that are likely to produce capital gains or losses. If homes, which are taxed only rarely because of special provisions in the tax law, are included in this group, about three-quarters of families own assets that might produce capital gains. Although most people do not sell any capital assets in a typical year— and those who do tend to have disproportionately high incomes— over the period 1979–88 more than a third of taxpayers realized at least one capital gain. And, in any given year, more than half of the tax returns with capital gains were filed by people with modest incomes (less than $50,000).

At the same time, wealthy people clearly own most of the assets that produce capital gains and realize a disproportionate share of such gains. Furthermore, most capital gains are reported by taxpayers who have many transactions and very large capital gains. Just over half of the wealth held in the form of capital gains assets other than homes is owned by families who have incomes of more than $100,000, and those families realize 70 percent or more of capital gains in a typical year. High-income families are more likely to realize capital gains than lower-income families, and the amount realized is many times larger than the typical gain realized by the rest of the population. In 1993, 80 percent of taxpayers with incomes of $200,000 or more realized a capital gain, compared with 15 percent of all taxpayers. The average gain for such taxpayers was $143,943, compared with an average of $7,883 for all taxpayers. Capital gains are likely to be much larger in 1998 after four years of extraordinary stock market growth. Between January 1994 and January 1998, the Standard and Poor's 500 index doubled.[1]

Capital gains are a much larger share of the income of people who have high incomes than that of people whose incomes are lower. Between 1979 and 1988 taxpayers with an average income of $200,000 or more earned 38 percent of that income in the form of capital gains; for the population as a whole, capital gains constituted only 6 percent of income.

As with other forms of income from capital, a large fraction of capital gains simply reflects inflation. Many capital assets are sold for less than their purchase price after adjusting for inflation, but their owners must pay tax on the gain created by inflation. That issue, too, is even more complex when examined closely, because the interaction of taxes and inflation penalizes other kinds of income from capital, such as interest and dividends, more than it penalizes capital gains.

To put matters in perspective, between 1954 and 1996 tax revenues from capital gains constituted more than 10 percent of total revenues from individual income taxes (4 percent of all tax revenues) only in one year: 1986.[2] The huge realizations in that year were an anomaly caused by the prospect of higher tax rates after the Tax Reform Act of 1986. Although taxes on capital gains loom large for a small fraction of taxpayers, they are a relatively minor component of total individual income tax receipts.

Who Owns Capital Gains Assets?

Although capital gains, and the resulting tax liability, are computed on the basis of income tax returns, data from individual returns do not fully reflect the distribution of those liabilities. People do not pay tax on capital gains until they sell assets, even though those assets are constantly gaining or losing value. From their tax returns, then, it appears that those who choose not to sell their assets in any given year are unaffected by the capital gains tax. Similarly, those who sell all or most of their holdings in any single year appear to be greatly affected by the tax. People who defer realizations of capital gains thus seem to have less income than they really do, whereas people who realize gains on assets that they have held for a long time have artificially inflated incomes. Data on realizations also typically understate the ownership of capital gains assets, because many capital gains are never taxed.

In 1992 about three-quarters of families in the United States owned stocks, bonds, business property, investment real estate, or a home (table 6-1). Any of those assets can produce capital gains or losses, although special rules exempt almost all gains on housing. Nearly half of all families own at least one capital gains asset apart from their home. Thus taxes on capital gains potentially affect a significant portion of the population.

Families that have higher incomes are more likely to hold capital gains assets than those with lower incomes. In 1992 about 30 percent of families with incomes of less than $20,000 owned capital gains assets (not including homes). The percentage increased to 50 percent for families who had incomes between $20,000 and $50,000, and to 70 percent for families with incomes between $50,000 and $100,000. More than 90 percent of families with incomes of $100,000 to $200,000 held such assets, while virtually all families with incomes of $200,000 or more held at least some capital gains assets.

The kinds of assets owned also vary with income. Fewer families with incomes of $200,000 or more held corporate stock than business property or real estate: 61 percent owned stock, 66 percent owned businesses, and 73 percent owned real estate. By contrast, about 32 percent of families with incomes between $50,000 and $100,000 held stock, while 30 percent owned real estate and 23 percent owned business property.

Ownership of capital gains assets varies with age, because people tend to accumulate assets over their working lives and sell them off during retirement. This life-cycle pattern is reflected in statistics on asset ownership. About 40 percent of families headed by someone younger than thirty-five held capital gains assets, compared with more than 50 percent of families headed by someone between thirty-five and sixty-four. The percentage falls slightly to 47 percent for families whose head is sixty-five or older.

Not surprisingly, the value of assets owned is highly correlated with income (since assets are an important source of income). In 1992 the

Table 6-1. Families Owning Capital Gains Assets, by Income and Age, 1992

Percent

Family characteristics	Percent of families	Capital gains assets other than homes							Principal residence	All capital gains assets
		Stocks	Taxable bonds	Tax-exempt bonds	Mutual funds	Business property	Investment real estate	All assets		
Family income (dollars)										
< 20,000	38.3	6.3	1.4	0.1	4.2	6.3	9.1	29.5	47.4	60.2
20,000–50,000	38.0	15.7	2.6	1.5	10.2	12.7	19.4	50.4	66.8	81.4
50,000–100,000	18.3	31.7	4.8	3.5	17.4	23.1	29.6	71.2	84.7	94.2
100,000–200,000	4.3	46.9	10.4	14.8	26.8	46.0	52.6	92.9	91.9	99.0
> 200,000	1.2	60.7	16.6	26.6	45.7	66.3	72.6	100.0	86.5	100.0
Age of family head										
< 35	25.8	10.6	1.1	0.4	5.1	10.6	8.2	39.9	36.9	59.3
35 to 44	22.8	19.5	1.7	1.2	10.1	19.1	16.7	52.0	64.5	77.8
45 to 54	16.2	18.4	3.3	3.3	9.4	18.4	25.1	51.8	75.4	83.0
55 to 64	13.2	21.5	3.0	2.9	15.8	18.2	35.1	59.5	77.6	86.8
65 and over	22.0	17.7	6.4	4.0	14.2	7.8	21.4	46.5	78.4	84.8
All families	. . .	16.9	3.0	2.2	10.4	14.2	19.4	48.6	63.9	76.6

Source: Congressional Budget Office tabulations of 1992 Survey of Consumer Finances.

1 percent of families whose incomes exceeded $200,000 held 22 percent of the value of capital gains assets, including homes (table 6-2). They owned 38 percent of business assets, 36 percent of corporate stock, and about 40 percent of bonds.

Families with incomes of more than $100,000 (approximately the top 5 percent) held 41 percent of all capital gains assets, and 61 percent of corporate stock. By comparison, families with income of less than $20,000 (or nearly 40 percent of all families), held 10 percent of assets: they held about 16 percent of the equity in homes, 7 percent of mutual funds, 6 percent of investment real estate, 5 percent of business assets, and 4 percent or less of stocks and bonds. Families with incomes of $20,000 to $100,000 (or just under 60 percent of families) held 62 percent of housing wealth but only 40 percent of other kinds of capital gains assets.

Who Realizes Capital Gains?

Although families with incomes of $100,000 or more own about half of the assets that produce capital gains, it does not necessarily follow that they realize half of the capital gains. Their share of taxable gains could be either smaller or larger than their share of assets. Taxes on capital gains provide all investors with an incentive to postpone realizing gains as long as possible, or to avoid them by donating appreciated assets to charity or holding until death. The incentive is greatest for investors who face the maximum tax rate on long-term capital gains of 20 percent, but that rate applies to most of the capital gains assets held by families. The ability to avoid tax may depend on the kinds of assets that people hold and how much money is at stake. As discussed in chapter 4, a simple strategy is to sell assets with capital losses to shelter from tax the capital gain on other assets. This strategy works best if the taxpayer owns a diversified portfolio of liquid assets, so it is easy to find assets with losses to shelter the gains and it does not cost very much to sell them. Such taxpayers are likely to also have higher incomes. More complex strategies can be used to avoid realizing a capital gain altogether, but they are costly to implement

Table 6-2. Distribution of Asset Holdings, by Income, 1992

Percent

Income (dollars)	Percent of families	Capital gains assets other than homes							Principal residence	All capital gains assets
		Stocks	Taxable bonds	Tax-exempt bonds	Mutual funds	Business property	Investment real estate	All assets		
< 20,000	38.3	3.8	4.0	0.3	6.8	4.8	6.4	5.7	15.8	9.7
20,000–50,000	39.0	12.0	14.1	12.9	24.6	15.5	20.1	17.2	32.2	23.3
50,000–100,000	18.3	24.7	22.2	17.3	28.7	20.8	23.3	23.1	30.2	25.9
100,000–200,000	4.3	23.9	19.3	27.8	18.9	21.1	21.6	21.4	14.7	18.8
> 200,000	1.2	35.6	40.4	41.7	21.0	37.7	28.5	32.6	7.0	22.4
Total	100.0	100.0	100.0	100.0	100.0	100.0	100.0	100.0	100.0	100.0

Source: Congressional Budget Office tabulations of 1992 Survey of Consumer Finances.

and therefore most attractive to people with high incomes. Alternatively, people with higher incomes may realize more capital gains and pay disproportionately more tax than would be suggested by wealth statistics, because they pick investments that pay more of their returns in the form of capital gains, or because they are more likely to trade frequently. In addition, there is some evidence that the rich earn higher rates of return than other people.[3]

The data are more consistent with the second hypothesis. People who have higher incomes realize a large fraction of the taxable capital gains. It is not true, however, that most of the people who have taxable capital gains have high incomes. In fact, most of the tax returns that report capital gains are filed by people whose incomes fall below $50,000 a year. But their capital gains are very small compared with those of taxpayers who have high incomes.

Evidence from a Panel

Most analyses of the distribution of capital gains by income are based on the Internal Revenue Service's annual compilation of tax returns, constructed by the Statistics of Income (SOI) division. The advantage of this data set is that it is timely and large: the tables in the following sections report data based on 104,357 tax returns filed in 1993.[4] The disadvantage is that "snapshots" can be misleading:[5] a taxpayer of modest income who sells a business may appear to have a very high income in that year; and a higher-income taxpayer who uses tax-minimizing strategies to avoid realizing taxable gains in years when his or her income is high will often appear to have low capital gains (as well as understated income). These factors tend to tilt the distribution in different directions: the first would allocate too many capital gains to higher-income taxpayers, the second too few. Thus it is not apparent how misleading annual snapshots are, or in what direction.

These influences can be better understood by looking at the same taxpayers over a ten-year period.[6] Economists have long recognized that lifetime or "permanent" income more accurately reflects an individual's well-being than annual income, especially when annual income is volatile. Capital gains are one of the most volatile components of annual taxable income. Data for computing lifetime income and capital gains do not exist, but average income and gains over ten years can be calculated using a panel of data from the tax returns of about 20,000 taxpayers who filed from 1979 to 1988. The panel was created by the Treasury's Office of Tax Analysis and the SOI division of the IRS.

That data set is somewhat out of date (only available through 1988), much smaller than the annual SOI, and less representative of the population than the SOI in the latter years, which is why the panel is not the basis for most official estimates of the distribution of taxes. But it does allow one to compare the perspective over the long term with annual snapshots based on the same data. In most years the quantitative distribution in these two cases is markedly different: higher-income people have a smaller share of capital gains in the longer-term picture. In qualitative terms, however, the strong positive relation between income and capital gains emerges in both the panel and annual data. With their other advantages of timeliness and accuracy, the annual data therefore remain a useful source of information about the distribution of income, including capital gains.

The evidence from the panel is also broadly consistent with the evidence from the data about wealth. About 49 percent of families owned capital gains assets (excluding housing) in 1992, according to the Federal Reserve Board's Survey of Consumer Finances (SCF). Nearly one-third of taxpayers reported a capital gain at least once during the ten years of the panel (table 6-3). If those taxpayers owned capital assets in the same proportion as families in the SCF, about two-thirds of them (32 percent divided by 49 percent) chose to sell at least some of them during the ten-year period. However, taxpayers are more likely to own capital gains assets than the rest of the population, because people who do not file tax returns (those excluded from the tax data but included in the SCF) have low incomes. Assuming that taxpayers are as likely to own capital gains assets as the SCF families whose incomes exceed $20,000, about 58 percent of taxpayers who owned capital gains assets chose to sell any of them over the ten-year period.

The likelihood of realizing a capital gain or loss is similar to the likelihood of owning a capital gains asset. Thus the probability of realizing a gain or loss increases steadily with income. Over the ten-year period of the panel, less than 20 percent of taxpayers with average incomes between $0 and $20,000 realized a capital gain. By contrast, 89 percent of taxpayers with average incomes between $100,000 and $200,000 realized at least one gain; 99 percent of taxpayers with average incomes greater than $200,000 reported a gain. At the same time, the wealth data showed that about 30 percent of families with incomes of $20,000 or less owned capital gains assets, whereas 93 percent of families with incomes between $100,000 and $200,000, and 100 percent of families with incomes of $200,000 or more owned such assets.[7]

Taxpayers who have higher incomes have larger gains, and they realize gains more frequently than lower-income taxpayers. Taxpayers with average incomes between $0 and $50,000 who realized a gain reported gain or loss in three years out of ten, on average. In the highest income brackets, gains were reported in six or seven years out of ten. The average gain (expressed in 1993 dollars) reported by taxpayers with gains and incomes of $50,000 or less was under $2,000, compared with $15,505 for taxpayers with incomes between $100,000 and $200,000, and $179,043 for taxpayers whose incomes were greater than $200,000.

About 0.3 percent of all taxpayers had negative total income over the ten years. They are clearly different from the other low-income people in the sample. Nearly three-quarters of them had a gain or loss over the ten-year period, and their average capital gain actually amounted to a loss of nearly $28,000. The taxpayers who realized a gain or loss did so in five years out of ten, on average. The frequency of gains makes these people resemble taxpayers who had incomes of between $75,000 and $100,000 rather than a low income. The category is probably a combination of taxpayers who had tax-shelter losses and taxpayers who had bad luck on investments. (Taxpayers whose only sources of income are wages, interest, and dividends cannot have negative income.)

Capital gains are a much larger share of income for people who have high incomes than for those who have low and moderate incomes. Capital gains make up 38 percent of income for people who

Table 6-3. People Who Realized Capital Gains between 1979 and 1988, by Average Income[a]

Average income (dollars)	Average gain (dollars)	Gain as percent of income	Tax units in income class with gain or loss (percent)	Taxpayers with gains Average gain (dollars)	Taxpayers with gains Gain as percent of income	Taxpayers with gains Average number of years with gains
> 0	−20,126	...	72	−27,874	...	5
0–10,000	13	0	10	128	2	3
10,000–20,000	202	1	19	1,052	7	3
20,000–30,000	323	1	27	1,201	5	3
30,000–40,000	674	2	36	1,881	5	3
40,000–50,000	707	2	42	1,671	4	3
50,000–75,000	1,554	3	56	2,786	5	4
75,000–100,000	4,856	6	78	6,256	7	5
100,000–200,000	13,276	11	89	15,505	12	6
> 200,000	177,045	38	99	179,041	38	7
All	2,015	6	32	6,250	12	4

Source: Congressional Budget Office tabulations of Treasury Statistics of Income (SOI) panel.

a. Average income is based on returns filed from 1979 to 1988. Income includes wages and salaries, interest, dividends, current-year capital gains, pensions, rents, royalties, and business and farm income. Gain is the sum of capital gains net of losses without regard for loss limits or losses carried over into 1979. All dollar amounts are in 1993 dollars, inflated by the consumer price index.

have incomes greater than $200,000, compared with 7 percent or less for people with incomes below $100,000. The percentage increases because people with higher incomes are more likely to have capital gains than people with lower incomes and to have larger capital gains when they realize them. For lower-income taxpayers who have capital gains at least once over the ten-year period, the gains constitute a larger share of their incomes: as much as 7 percent for taxpayers with incomes between $10,000 and $20,000.

Capital gains are a small part of income for most taxpayers of working age. For taxpayers who were younger than sixty-five in 1981 (the base year of the panel), wages constituted 83 percent of income (figure 6-1).[8] Capital gains averaged 5 percent, a slightly smaller share than interest and dividends and other forms of income, such as rents, royalties, and business income, which each made up about 6 percent of total income. People with incomes of $100,000 or less have relatively little income from capital—wages and salaries make up 86 percent to 90 percent of income—and much more of their capital income is in the form of interest, dividends, rents, royalties, and business income than capital gains. Capital gains are much more important for high-income people of working age, and wages much less important. For those under the age of sixty-five, capital gains contributed 3 percent to the incomes of taxpayers with incomes of $50,000 to $100,000, compared with 9 percent for taxpayers with incomes between $100,000 and $200,000, and 37 percent for those with incomes greater than $200,000. Wages decline similarly, from 86 percent of income for taxpayers with income of $50,000 to $100,000 to 44 percent of income for taxpayers in the highest-income group. Interest, dividends, and other forms of income also increase in importance, but much less than capital gains.

For older people (sixty-five and older in 1981), wages are a comparatively small portion of income (figure 6-1). Interest and dividends make up 44 percent of income on average. Capital gains contribute 14 percent, compared with about 19 percent from wages and salaries. Because many older people do not have wage income, capital gains are a larger share of income at all income levels than for younger taxpayers, constituting 16 percent of income for taxpayers with incomes

Figure 6-1. Composition of Income for Taxpayers

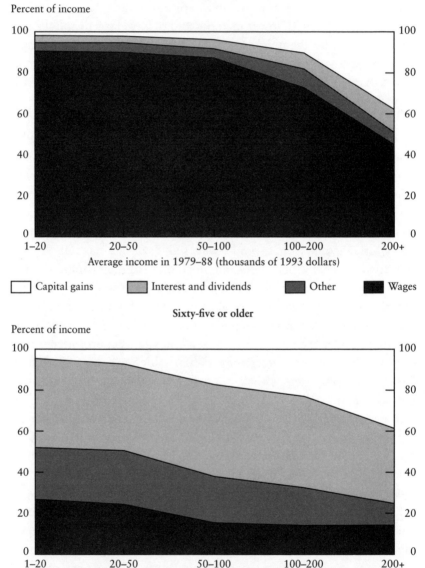

Under age sixty-five[a]

Percent of income

Capital gains   Interest and dividends   Other   Wages

Sixty-five or older

Percent of income

Average income in 1979–88 (thousands of 1993 dollars)

Source: Congressional Budget Office tabulations of the Treasury SOI panel.
a. Based on age in 1981, excluding returns for which age could not be determined.

between $50,000 and $100,000. The share of capital gains in the incomes of taxpayers with the highest incomes, however, is only slightly greater than for the younger taxpayers with high incomes—about 38 percent.

These patterns suggest that people with higher incomes, who also faced the highest tax rates, preferred capital gains assets, which were relatively lightly taxed. Middle-income people, facing lower tax rates, were much more willing to earn income in taxable form. Economists call this sorting of investment choices by tax status the "clientele effect." The theory is that clienteles form for different kinds of assets depending on their tax status: fully taxed assets such as dividend-paying stock and taxable bonds are held largely by untaxed or lightly taxed investors, while tax-preferred investments such as appreciating assets and tax-exempt bonds tend to be held by high-tax investors. Of course, factors other than taxes contribute to those differences. Older people, for instance, prefer to hold more liquid assets, which are more likely to pay out income in the form of interest and dividends than capital gains. Lower-income people are less inclined to bear the risk associated with many investments that pay returns in the form of capital gains. And they might have a stronger preference for current (rather than deferred) income than people with higher incomes.

Thus it is not surprising that even on the basis of the long-term perspective, more than half of capital gains are realized by the 1 percent of taxpayers who are in the highest income class (table 6-4). The 3 percent of taxpayers whose incomes (in 1993 dollars) averaged $100,000 or more over the ten years earned nearly three-quarters of the capital gains. It is also true, however, that over ten years most of the taxpayers who have gains have modest incomes (less than $50,000).

How Misleading Are Annual Snapshots?

For the most part, panel data are not available for the purpose of computing average incomes and capital gains. But the annual data may be misleading; compared with data from a longer time span, they overstate the percentage of gains earned by the people with the highest incomes and the losses incurred by those whose incomes are

Table 6-4. Distribution of Average Capital Gains, by Average Income, 1979–88ª

Percent

Average income (1993 dollars)	All tax units	All tax units that had a gain	Gains in income class
< 0	0	1	–3
0–10,000	15	5	0
10,000–20,000	26	15	3
20,000–30,000	18	15	3
30,000–40,000	13	14	4
40,000–50,000	10	13	3
50,000–75,000	12	20	9
75,000–100,000	4	9	9
100,000–200,000	2	6	16
> 200,000	1	2	57
All tax units	100	100	100

Source: Congressional Budget Office tabulations of Treasury SOI panel.
a. Income includes wages and salaries, interest, dividends, current-year capital gains, pensions, rents, royalties, and business and farm income. Gain is the sum of capital gains net of losses without regard for loss limits or losses carried over into 1979.

reported as negative. The percentage of capital gains in the extreme income categories varies considerably from year to year. Between 1979 and 1988 taxpayers who had annual incomes of $200,000 or more (in 1993 dollars) earned between 59 percent and 91 percent of capital gains, but taxpayers who had average incomes of this level earned only 57 percent of average capital gains over the entire ten-year period (table 6-5).

Data for 1986 to 1988 may be peculiar because of the Tax Reform Act of 1986. Realizations of capital gains were extraordinarily high in 1986 as taxpayers rushed to sell assets before the tax rate increased in 1987.[9] They were probably depressed in 1987 and 1988 because many assets that would have been sold in those years were sold in 1986 instead. If the years affected by the act (1986–88) are excluded, 52 percent of gains were earned by the people in the top income category, compared with 57 percent in the full ten-year panel.

Annual data often included larger losses than in the averages over the ten years of the panel. In October 1987, when the stock market declined sharply after a strong bull market earlier in the year, losses incurred by people who had negative incomes offset 20 percent of total net gains. In 1979, 1980, and 1988, losses offset from 14 percent to 18 percent of net gains, but the average losses incurred by taxpayers who had negative incomes over the whole ten years equaled only 3 percent of gains; except in 1986–88, such losses amounted to less than 2 percent of gains.

The annual snapshots present a similar qualitative picture. Consider the distribution of capital gains in 1984, the middle year of the panel, and the distribution based on the panel, with and without 1986–88 (figure 6-2). In 1984 somewhat more taxpayers had gains in the highest income levels, and fewer taxpayers with lower income had gains, but the correlation between the data for 1984 and the ten-year average is quite high. The Pearson correlation coefficient is 0.996 (where 1.0 indicates perfect correlation, and 0.0 indicates no relationship at all). Even for the anomalous year of 1987 (not shown on figure 6-2), the correlation is 0.985.

Some annual measures of the distribution of capital gains *are* misleading. Measures using wage level, for instance, are misleading because old people—many of whom are quite wealthy—have little or no wages (as is true of younger entrepreneurs whose income arises from self-employment rather than wages; see box 6-1). Some analysts have advocated removing capital gains from income, but this too can vastly understate the income of people whose income arises in large part—or in total—from capital. Recall that for people with the highest incomes, capital gains make up 37 percent of their *average* income over ten years (figure 6-1.) Excluding capital gains would thus understate their average income by more than one-third.

Evidence from Annual Tax Returns

Because of the limitations cited earlier, it is useful to look at data drawn from the full SOI, which is larger, more current, and more representative of the behavior of all taxpayers in a single year. In 1993, 76 percent of capital gains were realized by the 3 percent of families and individuals whose incomes exceeded $100,000 (table 6-6).[10] That

Table 6-5. Percentage Distribution of Capital Gains, by Annual and Average Incomes, 1979–88[a]

Income (dollars)	1979	1980	1981	1982	1983	1984	1985	1986	1987	1988	Average Ten years	Average Seven years
< 0	-14	-15.8	-0.1	-0.4	-0.1	-0.7	-3.7	-5.0	-20.3	-17.7	-3.3	-1.6
0	0	0	0	0	0	0	0	0	0	0	0	0
1–10,000	-1.0	-0.4	-0.8	0.4	-0.3	0.1	0.0	-0.1	-1.2	-0.5	0.1	0.2
10,000–20,000	1.0	0	1.9	1.9	1.0	0.7	0.4	0.6	1.4	-0.5	2.6	2.0
20,000–30,000	1.8	1.8	2.3	2.9	2.7	2.3	1.2	0.6	2.2	1.1	2.9	3.9
30,000–40,000	4.1	3.7	1.2	4.1	1.9	2.7	2.6	1.2	2.0	1.5	4.4	4.4
40,000–50,000	3.0	3.2	3.7	3.1	1.8	1.6	2.3	1.0	3.5	0.7	3.4	4.0
50,000–75,000	10.6	10.3	6.7	7.5	10.7	5.6	6.0	4.0	5.6	4.4	9.0	10.7
75,000–100,000	8.4	10.6	8.7	5.3	7.6	6.4	6.0	5.3	7.4	5.1	8.5	6.7
100,000–200,000	21.9	19.8	17.6	14.6	15.5	18.4	16.5	13.1	22.0	15.1	15.7	18.0
> 200,000	64.2	66.8	58.8	60.6	59.2	62.9	68.5	79.3	77.4	90.8	56.8	51.6
Total	100.0	100.0	100.0	100.0	100.0	100.0	100.0	100.0	100.0	100.0	100.0	100.0

Source: Congressional Budget Office tabulations of Treasury SOI panel.

a. Average income is based on returns filed from 1979 to 1988. Income includes wages, interest, dividends, current-year capital gains, rents, royalties, and other business income.

Figure 6-2. Share of Realized Capital Gains, by Income

Percent of gains

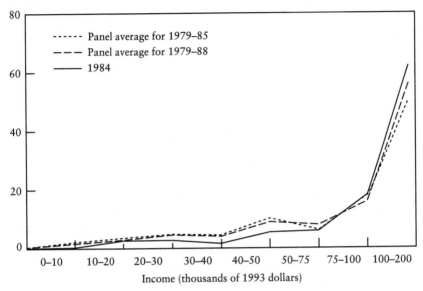

Income (thousands of 1993 dollars)

Source: Congressional Budget Office tabulations of the Treasury SOI panel.

is only slightly higher than the 72 percent of gains realized by tax-payers in the panel who had average incomes of $100,000 or more (in 1993 dollars), but this similarity may be coincidental given the larger variations between annual and panel data described in the previous section. More striking, less than one-half as many people realized gains in that single year as they did over the ten-year panel. Only 15 percent of returns in 1993 reported a capital gain, compared with 32 percent in the panel. As in the panel, the percentage increases with income, although even in the highest income category, only four out of five taxpayers reported a gain or loss in a single year (compared with 99 percent in the panel). Also, as in the panel results, most of the tax-payers who had gains had incomes of $50,000 or less.

Another way to measure distribution is to look at the size of gains realized. Most capital gains are realized by a relatively small number

Box 6-1. Misleading Statistics

As noted in the text, the annual distribution of capital gains by income is somewhat misleading, although the qualitative picture does not change markedly when data over many years are used. It does change greatly, however, when capital gains are distributed by wages. In 1993, 38 percent of capital gains reported on joint returns were realized by taxpayers with wages of $10,000 or less, 50 percent by returns with wages of $40,000 or less (see the following table). This statistic leads some to conclude that most capital gains are realized by people of really modest means.

This inference is totally specious. Upon further examination, one can see that 29 percent of gains are on returns with *zero* wages. These are not poor people who are cashing in their stocks and bonds to avoid sleeping on heating grates. Seventy percent of them are retired people who are augmenting their social security with accumulated savings, some of which are capital gains assets. Fifty-seven percent of capital gains among the elderly were on returns with zero wages. The nonelderly in this category are self-employed or earn all their income from capital (including capital gains). The average capital gain for people with zero wages is actually higher than the population average. This does not mean that capital gains are progressively distributed with

of investors who have many transactions and large gains. In 1993, 647 returns reported total capital gains of more than $10 million. This group accounted for 12 percent of all capital gains. Less than 0.1 percent of returns showed capital gains greater than $1 million, but they accounted for nearly one-third of gains (table 6-7). More than one-half of capital gains were reported on the 0.5 percent of returns with capital gains of $200,000 or more. Although most returns with capital gains reported small gains (less than $10,000), they accounted for only 15 percent of all capital gains.

income. It means that wages vastly understate well-being for many people with substantial capital income.

Although somewhat less egregious, it is also misleading to look at the distribution of capital gains by income net of capital gains. For many wealthy people, capital gains are an important and recurring source of income.

Distribution of Capital Gains by Wages and Salaries, Joint Returns

Percent unless otherwise specified

Wages and salaries	Returns with gains	Gains		Average returns with gains (dollars)
		All ages	65 and over	
0	24	29	57	11,845
1–10,000	10	9	13	8,691
10,000–20,000	6	5	5	7,774
20,000–30,000	6	3	2	5,016
30,000–40,000	7	4	2	5,018
40,000–50,000	8	3	1	3,794
50,000–75,000	17	7	2	3,662
75,000–100,000	9	5	2	5,090
100,000–200,000	9	11	5	11,646
> 200,000	3	24	11	68,584
All returns	100	100	100	9,593

Source: 1993 SOI.

The Importance of Isolated Transactions

Although many of the tax returns with capital gains list only one or two transactions, they account for only a small fraction of the gains realized. Most capital gains are reported by wealthy investors who hold many assets and sell assets frequently. In 1993, 38 percent of returns with capital gains reported only one transaction (table 6-8). About 56 percent of returns with gains reported two or fewer. But these returns had much smaller than average gains and so contributed

Table 6-6. Distribution of Capital Gains, by Income Class, 1993ᵃ

| Income (dollars) | Returns (thousands) | Percent | | | Average gains for returns with gains (dollars) |
		Returns in class with gains	Returns in class	Gains in class	
< 0	1,232	37	3	–7	–20,141
0–10,000	32,214	8	15	1	512
10,000–20,000	24,644	10	14	3	1,769
20,000–30,000	17,746	13	13	4	2,370
30,000–40,000	12,710	15	11	4	2,856
40,000–50,000	8,717	19	9	4	3,191
50,000–75,000	10,865	27	17	9	4,149
75,000–100,000	3,318	41	8	6	6,194
100,000–200,000	2,405	58	8	14	14,482
> 200,000	752	80	3	62	143,943
All classes	114,603	15	100	100	7,883

Source: Congressional Budget Office tabulations of 1993 SOI.

a. Income is defined to be independent of tax law. It includes wages and salaries, interest, dividends, current year capital gains, rents, royalties, and other business income. Gains are net capital gains before carryovers and loss limits.

relatively little to overall capital gains. Returns with a single transaction accounted for only 7 percent of gains. Returns with one or two transactions accounted for 14 percent of the total. The 19 percent that reported more than five transactions, however, accounted for 59 percent of all capital gains.

Many of the isolated transactions were probably capital gains distributions from mutual funds, which grew in importance between 1985 and 1993. In 1985 less than 2 percent of net capital gains realized were from mutual fund distributions.[11] By 1993 they accounted for 7 percent of the total. In 1985 less than 5 percent of transactions were capital gains distributions. In 1993 they represented 9 percent of transactions.

Other Evidence of Tax Avoidance

Tables 6-1 to 6-8 contain little evidence to indicate that the rich are avoiding more than their share of the capital gains tax. If anything, the

Table 6-7. Distribution of Capital Gains, by Size of Gain, 1993 Returns with Gain or Loss

Net capital gain per return (thousands of dollars)	Returns (thousands)	Share of returns (percent)	Share of gains (percent)	Average gains (thousands of dollars)
< 0	2,927	17	–15	–7
0–10	12,749	72	15	2
10–20	946	5	10	14
20–30	358	2	6	24
30–40	204	1	5	35
40–50	121	1	4	45
50–75	164	1	7	60
75–100	79	0	5	86
100–200	103	1	10	140
200–500	55	0	12	309
500–1,000	17	0	8	688
1,000–2,000	7	0	7	1,370
2,000–5,000	4	0	8	3,011
5,000–10,000	1	0	5	6,831
> 10,000	1	0	12	23,798
All returns	17,736	100	100	8

Source: Congressional Budget Office tabulations of 1993 SOI.

opposite appears to be true. The top 5 percent of the population owns about half of capital gains assets (table 6-2) and realizes an even larger share of taxable capital gains (table 6-3). Nonetheless, people with high incomes have the strongest incentive to avoid capital gains tax, not only because they have large gains and face the highest tax rates, but also because they are best able to pay for expert advice to implement complicated tax-avoidance strategies. Thus it is possible that the gains rich people realize are only a tiny share of their total gains.

Notwithstanding the pattern reflected in the distributional tables, evasion by the rich appears to be supported by anecdotal evidence. In the most notorious anecdote, Esteé Lauder borrowed shares of stock in her eponymous business from relatives and sold those, instead of the shares that she owned. The plan was to repay the borrowed stock at her death, thereby deferring the technical realization of gain until death, when it would be tax-free. This kind of short-against-the-box transaction allowed rich investors to realize their gains without actually

Table 6-8. Distribution of Capital Gains, by Number of Transactions, 1993ᵃ

| Number of transactions | | Percent | | Average gain per return (dollars) |
	Returns	Returns with gains	Gains	
0	87.4	0	0	0
1	4.7	37.6	7.3	1,794
2	2.3	18.5	7.1	3,541
3–5	3.2	25.3	26.5	9,655
6–10	1.6	12.5	20.4	15,003
11–25	0.6	4.9	21.0	39,472
26–50	0.1	0.9	6.8	73,272
> 50	0	0.4	10.9	250,043
All returns	100.0	100.0	100.0	9,202

Source: Congressional Budget Office tabulations of 1993 sales of capital assets.
a. The average gain per return is higher in these data than in the 1993 Statistics of Income. For a discussion, see U.S. Congressional Budget Office, "Perspectives on the Ownership of Capital Assets and the Realization of Capital Gains." Capital gains distributions are considered to be a single transaction.

triggering any tax liability. In Ms. Lauder's case, the deal saved her millions of dollars of capital gains tax.

The Esteé Lauder deal and some similarly egregious abuses attracted so much negative publicity that Congress outlawed them in the 1997 tax act. Nonetheless, some analysts believe that wealthy people will be able to avoid the capital gains tax no matter how many restrictions Congress imposes. Princeton economist David Bradford rearked on the futility of anti–capital gains tax avoidance provisions: "The simple fact is that anyone sitting on a big pot of money today probably isn't paying capital-gains taxes and the government can adopt rule after rule after rule—but the people who will get stuck paying capital-gains taxes will be the ordinary investors who own mutual funds."[12]

Obviously, tax avoidance by the wealthy raises concerns about fairness. A tax that the rich can avoid but that middle-income people get stuck paying is obviously unfair. Also, the apparent fact that some high-income people pay a great deal of tax while other people in similar circumstances avoid it violates a fundamental principle of taxation. Furthermore, capital gains tax avoidance is not without cost. Financial advisers charge substantial fees to manage complicated tax dodges. In effect, those fees are a tax that generates no revenue for the govern-

Figure 6-3. Distribution of Realized and Accrued Gains on Stock, by Income[a]

Percent of all gains

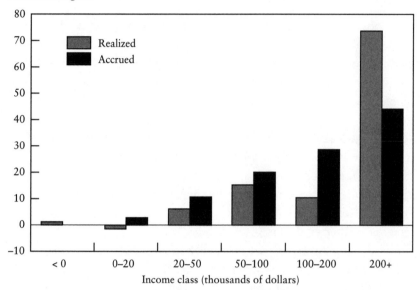

Income class (thousands of dollars)

Source: Auerbach, Burman, and Siegel, "Capital Gains Taxation and Tax Avoidance."
a. Accrued gains are based on the 1992 Survey of Consumer Finances; realized gains are the average capital gain on corporate stock between 1988 and 1994 from the IRS, sales of capital assets.

ment, and the service they produce has no value except in relation to the tax system. This is a quintessential example of a deadweight loss. The financial advisers could presumably be producing intrinsically valuable goods or services were they not engaged in tax avoidance.

Empirical evidence suggests, however, that the anecdotes are not characteristic of most high-income taxpayers' behavior. The first point to mention is that high-income people pay a disproportionate amount of tax, not only in relation to their ownership of capital assets but also to their accrual of capital gains. In 1992 (the only year for which such data are available) the average realizations of capital gains on corporate stock increased faster with income than accruals (figure 6-3). Between 1988 and 1994 taxpayers with an income of $100,000 or more realized an average of 87 percent of the gains on corporate stock, whereas their accruals accounted for only 70 percent of gains.

Although part of the discrepancy may be a data problem, there is no evidence in these data that high-income people are realizing gains at a lower rate than people with modest incomes.[13]

Second, capital gains appear to be fairly unresponsive to permanent changes in tax rates (see chapter 4). It may be that most people find the costs of avoidance so high that they do not do it. Otherwise, as tax rates fell, one would expect more capital gains to be realized as more and more avoidance strategies became unprofitable. Further evidence consistent with this explanation arises from the fact that capital gains realizations are extremely responsive when the cost of avoidance is low. As discussed in chapter 4, the timing of capital gains is highly sensitive to anticipated changes in tax rates, such as the increase in tax rates that was legislated in 1986 but did not become effective until 1987.[14] The occurrence of high transitory elasticity is further evidence.[15]

Third, most taxpayers do not shelter their gains with losses, which is a relatively simple avoidance strategy.[16] A 1986 study showed that although high-income taxpayers with capital gains are more likely to be in a net loss position than lower-income taxpayers with gains, the vast majority of people at every income level have positive net capital gains.[17] Avoidance appears to increase with income and wealth, but affects only a minority of taxpayers at all levels.

An analysis based on post-TRA86 data produced similar results.[18] A class of "sophisticated" investors, defined as those who engage in short sales, options, and futures trading, were found to be significantly more likely to be in a net loss position than other investors. Furthermore, high-income taxpayers showed considerable heterogeneity in their tastes for avoidance.

Perhaps more important, successful tax avoidance by this measure was difficult to maintain. Most taxpayers who sheltered their gains from tax in a given year realized positive net gains within a year or two. Thus the tax shelter simply resulted in the deferral of tax for a short period of time, not a permanent deferral as would be the case if the taxpayer never realized a positive gain until death. Again, some taxpayers were prone to remain in the net loss position for a longer period of time, but the overwhelming majority in every tax bracket paid rates close to the statutory rates, even after accounting for the benefits of tax sheltering.

All in all, it seems that capital gains tax avoidance was not rampant, even at the relatively high tax rates in effect after TRA86. However, it may have been increasing over time.[19] Complicated avoidance strategies may take a while to catch on, so avoidance by the rich might have become more prevalent if capital gains tax rates had not been cut in 1997. Of course, the change in rules concerning effective realizations would have had the opposite effect, no matter what had been done to tax rates.

The Effects of Inflation

In time, inflation tends to erode the value of assets. As a result, many realized capital gains are actually capital losses after correcting for inflation. The aggregate sale price of capital gains assets in 1993 was substantially less than the aggregate inflation-adjusted purchase price, net of depreciation allowances. Before adjustment for inflation, capital assets other than bonds generated net realized capital gains of $71.9 billion (table 6-9).[20] In real terms, however, they produced a net loss of $19.4 billion. Taxpayers realized real losses at most income levels, but the losses were proportionately greater at the lower income levels.[21]

Under current law, taxpayers are not permitted to deduct net capital losses in excess of $3,000. Losses beyond that must be carried over to future years. The loss limit applied under current law increased taxable gains by about 12 percent, to $81.4 billion in 1993. Such a loss limit applied to real capital gains and losses would make the net taxable capital gain positive, despite the fact that the average asset has a loss. The $19.4 billion real loss would turn into a $39.6 billion taxable gain after applying the loss limit.

Under current law, the loss limit is necessary to prevent taxpayers from using capital losses as a tax shelter for ordinary income, while endlessly deferring tax on assets with capital gains. Such a limit would be even more important if asset sales were indexed for inflation,

Table 6-9. Nominal and Real Capital Gains for All Assets except Bonds, by Income, 1993[a]

Millions of dollars unless otherwise specified

Income (dollars)	Returns (thousands)	Transactions (thousands)	Nominal		Real	
			No loss limit	Current-law loss limit	No loss limit	Current-law loss limit
< 0	155	606	-67	1,203	-3,388	468
1–10,000	1,619	3,560	-685	218	-6,009	-1,048
10,000–20,000	986	2,957	1,761	2,101	-3,809	99
20,000–30,000	735	1,858	2,735	3,023	-172	1,598
30,000–40,000	962	2,726	1,514	1,897	-3,190	-660
40,000–50,000	965	2,238	2,842	3,510	-4,496	444
50,000–75,000	1,971	6,272	6,285	7,505	-4,283	2,531
75,000–100,000	789	3,363	1,541	2,349	-2,887	338
100,000–200,000	1,075	6,333	18,940	20,326	-160	9,503
> 200,000	563	7,371	37,020	39,287	9,036	26,227
Total	9,821	37,084	71,886	81,419	-19,358	39,550

Source: Congressional Budget Office tabulations of 1993 sales of capital assets.

a. Income includes wages and salaries, interest, dividends, current-year capital gains, pensions, rents, royalties, and business and farm income. Transactions with missing buy years or inconsistent sales price information were excluded. The excluded returns are not likely to be a random subsample of the population. For example, assets with missing buy years are more likely to be those held for a long time.

because there would be so many more assets with real losses.[22] The possibility for sheltering substantial amounts of other income from tax would be immense. Subject to the loss limit, the average taxpayer in most income categories has positive real capital gains.

Under indexing, the basis (or purchase price) of capital gains assets is adjusted for inflation before capital gain is computed. Thus, if an asset was purchased for $1,000 and sold for $3,000 and the price level had doubled over the intervening period, the adjusted basis would be increased by indexing from $1,000 to $2,000 to account for the doubling in prices; indexed capital gain would be $1,000 ($3,000 minus $2,000). Australia and the United Kingdom index capital gains for inflation. The U. S. tax code does not index capital gains but does index tax rate schedules and several other provisions.[23]

The imposition of a loss limit has a much greater effect on taxable gains when they are indexed than when they are not. Many taxpayers who have positive net gains have substantial losses after indexing, and anyone with a nominal loss has an even greater real loss. Most indexing proposals would limit the indexing adjustment on individual assets to the amount of the nominal capital gain. Under such a limit, nominal gains could not be converted to losses by indexing, and losses would not be indexed at all. The amount of the indexing adjustment would be only a fraction of the cost of inflation for the assets with real losses.

The indexing adjustment for depreciable business assets is inexact because economic depreciation cannot be measured accurately. Corporate stock does not depreciate, so indexing provides an exact measure of real appreciation in that case (assuming the measure of price inflation is accurate). Overall, real capital gains on corporate stock were slightly positive in 1993 (table 6-10). As in previous years, taxpayers in the highest income groups tended to earn higher real returns. In part that may be because people who have lower incomes, especially senior citizens, are more likely to hold stocks that pay out their income in the form of dividends. Thus, as in the case of business assets, it is not surprising that they are more likely to realize losses after adjustment for inflation. People in the highest income bracket have substantial positive real capital gains, even before imposition of a loss limit.

Table 6-10. Nominal and Real Capital Gains from Corporate Stock, by Income, 1993[a]

Millions of dollars unless otherwise specified

Income (dollars)	Returns (thousands)	Transactions (thousands)	Nominal		Real	
			No loss limit	Current-law loss limit	No loss limit	Current-law loss limit
< 0	80	297	-146	578	-583	281
1–10,000	920	2,199	-855	-143	-4,831	-791
10,000–20,000	489	1,750	813	1,126	-2,364	128
20,000–30,000	318	672	197	273	-250	19
30,000–40,000	498	1,417	202	458	-1,326	-207
40,000–50,000	530	1,343	107	671	-612	159
50,000–75,000	1,189	3,768	4,186	5,222	1,097	2,752
75,000–100,000	494	2,173	90	503	-982	56
100,000–200,000	833	4,556	4,590	5,135	-1,184	2,945
> 200,000	380	5,731	23,181	24,775	11,080	21,279
Total	5,732	23,907	32,363	38,597	45	26,620

Source: Congressional Budget Office tabulations of 1993 sales of capital assets.

a. Income includes wages and salaries, interest, dividends, current-year capital gains, pensions, rents, royalties, and business and farm income. Transactions with missing buy years or inconsistent sales price information were excluded.

Tables 6-9 and 6-10 overstate the effects of inflation on total capital gains. Taxpayers have an incentive to accelerate the realization of losses and defer the realization of gains. That means the gains on assets people sell will typically be much smaller than the gains on assets people hold. The computed inflation adjustment is based on the consumer price index, which some analysts believe overstates inflation. A correct inflation index would produce a smaller adjustment. That is, the part of capital gains that reflects inflation may be substantially overstated in the tables. Nevertheless, capital gains, like other returns from capital, are taxed even when the apparent return represents nothing but inflation.

The Distribution of the Tax on Capital Gains

Who benefited from the recent cut in tax rates on capital gains? An obvious place to look for the answer to that question is among those paying the tax before it was cut. The more contentious issue is how to quantify the effects of the tax change. Some contend that the correct measure of who gains and by how much is the change in tax liability. This measure is misleading because people can choose when to realize a capital gain. If a lot of people decide to sell assets that they would have held in the absence of the tax change, they might end up paying as much tax as they did before the tax cut, even though they are clearly much better off.

Tax Burden before the 1997 Tax Cut

In 1993, 17.7 million taxpayers realized $140 billion of capital gains (table 6-11). After adding losses carried over from previous years and subtracting current losses in excess of the $3,000 limit (which are carried forward to later years), $144 billion of capital gain was included in taxable income. Individuals paid $33 billion in tax on those capital gains.[24] By comparison, in that same year the federal government collected $503 billion in individual income taxes from all sources. The tax on capital gains therefore amounted to 7 percent of the total. The

Table 6-11. Distribution of Taxes Paid on Capital Gains, by Income, 1993[a]

Millions unless otherwise specified

Income (dollars)	Number of returns	Current year gains	Taxable gains	Tax on gains	Percent of gains	Percent of tax
< 0	0.5	–9,285	240	–62	–6.6	–0.2
1–10,000	2.7	1,393	1,778	154	1.0	0.5
10,000–20,000	2.4	4,292	4,226	558	3.1	1.7
20,000–30,000	2.2	5,303	5,194	786	3.8	2.4
30,000–40,000	2.0	5,584	5,247	941	4.0	2.8
40,000–50,000	1.6	5,234	5,169	1,020	3.7	3.1
50,000–75,000	2.9	12,217	11,664	2,557	8.7	7.7
75,000–100,000	1.4	8,418	7,994	1,842	6.0	5.6
100,000–200,000	1.4	20,173	19,187	4,645	14.4	14.0
> 200,000	0.6	86,509	83,438	20,675	61.9	62.4
Total	17.7	139,837	144,130	33,115	100.0	100.0

Source: Congressional Budget Office tabulations of 1993 SOI and CBO tax model.

a. Income includes wages and salaries, interest, dividends, current-year capital gains, pensions, rents, royalties, and business and farm income. Current-year capital gains are capital gains less capital losses reported in 1993. Taxable gains include losses carried over from prior years but exclude net losses in excess of the $3,000 limit, which must be carried over to later years. Taxes are computed by comparing the tax liability with and without gains.

tax on capital gains for those who reported it amounted to 14 percent of their total income tax liability.

The distribution of tax liability attributable to capital gains is more concentrated at high income levels than the distribution of capital gains, because marginal tax rates increase with income. Taxpayers who have lower incomes faced marginal tax rates of 0 percent or 15 percent in 1993, whereas middle- and upper-income taxpayers faced the 28 percent maximum tax rate. Because almost all capital gains were realized by people in the 28 percent tax bracket, however, the difference is small. In 1993 taxpayers who had incomes of more than $200,000 realized 61.9 percent of the capital gains and paid 62.4 percent of the tax (table 6-11). By contrast, taxpayers who had incomes between $0 and $20,000 realized 4.1 percent of the gains, and paid 2.2 percent of the tax.

The marginal effective tax rate on capital gains—that is, the additional tax attributable to capital gains as a percentage of capital

Table 6-12. Distribution of Tax Liability, by Income and Age, 1993ᵃ

Percent

Income (dollars)	Effective tax rate			Tax on gains as percentage of all income tax		
	All taxpayers	Under 65	65 and older	All taxpayers	Under 65	65 and older
< 0	0.7	0.7	0.7	−0.8	−0.6	−1.8
1–10,000	11.0	10.8	11.7	1.8	2.0	1.3
10,000–20,000	13.0	12.8	13.2	2.4	1.3	6.8
20,000–30,000	14.8	14.3	15.4	1.9	1.0	7.3
30,000–40,000	16.8	14.8	18.9	1.9	0.9	11.5
40,000–50,000	19.5	17.7	21.7	2.2	1.2	11.6
50,000–75,000	20.9	20.4	21.8	2.8	1.8	14.6
75,000–100,000	21.9	21.5	22.7	3.8	2.7	17.3
100,000–200,000	23.0	22.5	24.1	6.9	5.1	21.7
> 200,000	23.9	23.6	24.9	17.9	15.8	31.1
All	23.7	23.5	24.2	6.6	5.2	17.5

Source: Congressional Budget Office tabulations of 1993 SOI and CBO tax model.

a. Income includes wages and salaries, interest, dividends, current-year capital gains, pensions, rents, royalties, and business and farm income. Capital gains are before carryover and loss limit. Taxes are computed by comparing the tax liability with and without the capital gains in adjusted gross income; in other words, capital gains are stacked last. Age is for the first listed social security number on joint returns.

gains—reflects the progressivity of the income tax. Taxpayers who had an income of less than $10,000 in 1993 paid an average of 11 percent of their capital gains in tax (table 6-12). The proportion increased to a maximum of about 24 percent for taxpayers in the highest income categories. It never reached the statutory maximum rate of 28 percent, because some taxpayers had losses and deductions that lowered their taxable income (before capital gains) below the threshold for the 28 percent bracket.

Effective tax rates vary a great deal among taxpayers at the highest income levels. Some taxpayers faced a maximum effective tax rate higher than 28 percent, as discussed in chapter 2. Many taxpayers who have incomes of more than $200,000 faced effective tax rates of 29.2 percent, because of the phaseout of itemized deductions that affects many taxpayers with higher incomes. A few face even higher tax rates because of other provisions, such as the partial taxation of social security benefits, which is phased in when income exceeds a certain amount. For example, taxpayers whose income excluding capital gains is below the threshold for taxation of social security may find that realizing capital gains subjects some of their social security benefits to tax. (This provision does not raise effective tax rates for taxpayers whose income before capital gains is high enough that all social security benefits would be subject to the partial tax.) Some taxpayers faced lower tax rates because they had carried over capital losses from previous years that sheltered current-year capital gains from tax, or business losses and other deductions that put them in lower tax brackets.

People of working age generally face lower tax rates on capital gains than do older people, because they have more exemptions and deductions and are usually not subject to the tax on social security benefits. Taxpayers over the age of sixty-five with incomes between $30,000 and $50,000 paid four percentage points more in tax on their capital gains than younger taxpayers with the same incomes primarily because of the social security provision. For taxpayers at other income levels, the difference averaged less than two percentage points.

Taxes on capital gains are an increasingly important part of total tax liability at higher incomes. For taxpayers whose incomes were less than $50,000 in 1993, taxes on capital gains were less than 3 percent of their total income tax liability. At the highest income levels, they were much more significant. For people who had incomes of more than $200,000, the tax on capital gains accounted for an average of 18 percent of their total income tax.

Taxes on capital gains are a much larger share of total income taxes for taxpayers over the age of sixty-four. They averaged 18 percent, compared with 5 percent for those under sixty-five. This difference arises because capital gains are a much larger share of income for the elderly (figure 6-1) and they are taxed at higher rates. Taxes on capital gains were 31 percent of total income taxes for taxpayers over sixty-four whose incomes exceed $200,000, compared with 16 percent for taxpayers under sixty-five.

Distribution of Changes in Tax

When taxes on capital gains are cut, the people holding the assets that generate those gains are made better off. If they made no change in their plans, they would gain a windfall equal to the tax savings on the assets they sell. Thus the static measure of change in tax—that is, assuming no behavioral response—is a lower bound on the gain to individuals.

In fact, people choose to realize more capital gains at lower tax rates (this is called the unlocking effect). Presumably, they do this because it makes them better off than they would be if their behavior were unchanged. But the additional realizations increase their tax payments compared with the static case. Ironically, the more distortionary the tax is—that is, the more the tax deters people from making the trades they want to make—the less their tax payments will decrease as a result of the tax cut. In the extreme, if the elasticity of realizations with respect to taxes is greater than one, people's tax payments can increase if the tax rate is cut. Clearly, this increase in tax payments does not indicate that they are worse off. Indeed, the opposite is true. If people's response to taxes is highly elastic, the benefit is much greater than the static revenue gain (see appendix E).

The correct way to measure the benefit of the tax change is to look at the distribution of static revenue losses (benefit from tax cuts to the individuals) and make an upward adjustment for the gain from the unlocking effect. This latter adjustment is hard to do accurately and in any event is likely to be quantitatively small in relation to the static revenue change.[25] For that reason, the Treasury's Office of Tax Analysis (OTA) distributes the static tax change, as Congress's Joint Committee on Taxation (JCT) did until 1994. This measure is understood to be a lower bound on the gain to individuals of a capital gains tax cut.

The Treasury and Joint Committee on Taxation do not typically publish estimates of the distribution of effects from a single provision. For that reason, the best gauge of the distribution of tax benefits from an across-the-board reduction in the taxation of gains is the distribution of taxes paid shown in table 6-11.[26] In other words, the benefit of across-the-board tax reductions such as the TRA97 are likely to be even more skewed with income than the distribution of realized capital gains.

The tax changes after accounting for behavioral responses would be much smaller, especially at the relatively high elasticities used by OTA and the JCT. It would be wrong to assume that these numbers have anything to do with the gains to individuals from cutting taxes. Like the static numbers, the dynamic estimates understate the gain to individuals from cutting rates, but the understatement is (at least) an order of magnitude larger than it is using the static estimates. In fact, if the capital gains realization elasticity is greater than 1, this measure will actually show an increase in tax burden even though taxpayers have been made much better off by the tax cut (see appendix E). The high elasticity indicates that taxpayers have been extremely constrained by capital gains taxes, so the reduction in rates is especially valuable to them. But showing the benefit in terms of changes in taxes paid after behavioral responses makes it look as though the taxpayers have been made worse off. This is totally misleading.

INDEXING CAPITAL GAINS FOR INFLATION

This chapter is the first of three that examine alternative ways of taxing capital gains. Each alternative is assessed in terms of its efficiency, equity, and simplicity, the core principles of public finance. Tax equity and simplicity mean the same thing for capital gains as they do for other forms of income: treat people in similar circumstances the same way, tax those with more ability to pay more heavily than those with lesser ability, and make the tax system relatively easy to comply with and administer. Efficiency is somewhat more difficult to judge, however, because it must be seen in the context of all the other constraints in the tax system. If the system features a separate unintegrated corporate income tax, one objective of capital gains tax policy will be to mitigate the double taxation of corporate earnings. If capital gains must be taxed when realized rather than as they accrue, then another objective will be to reduce lock-in. Yet another will be to avoid distorting people's portfolio decisions, which means that the disparity in tax treatment of different kinds of assets should be minimized and the tax law should not discourage risk-taking. And capital gains tax policy should take care not to encourage the formation of tax shelters. This chapter lays out the main option left on the table after the enactment of the Tax Relief Act of 1997, namely, to index capital gains for inflation.

Nine Out of Ten Economists *Can* Be Wrong

Indexing may be the most misunderstood aspect of capital gains taxation. Many analysts who oppose a reduced tax rate on capital gains because of concerns about tax sheltering and equity believe that indexation is a sensible reform. The argument for indexing is appealing on its face: capital gains represent inflation for the most part; many other components of the tax system are indexed; therefore indexing gains could achieve both fairness and economic efficiency.

The fallacy in this argument is that the "correct" tax treatment of capital gains depends on how other kinds of capital income are taxed. But taxes on other kinds of capital income—interest, dividends, rents, and royalties—cannot be deferred and thus are more affected by inflation than are the taxes on capital gains (see figure 4-1). Indexing would simply tilt the playing field even further in favor of assets that pay capital gains, a result that is obviously neither more fair nor more efficient. In addition, indexing would create the same kinds of incentives for inefficient tax shelters as a preferential rate.

At the same time, indexing has some advantages. Most notably, it would reduce—although not eliminate—the risk of additional tax liability due to unexpected inflation from investments that produce capital gains. The benefits of indexation are also much less skewed toward high-income taxpayers than a rate cut because the typical investor with moderate income has smaller real capital gains—that is, after removing the effects of inflation—than do high-income investors.

Up until 1997 much of the debate surrounding indexing centered on its advantages over a partial exclusion for capital gains, as had been in effect before 1987. Then Congress decided to cut rates on capital gains but declined to enact either an exclusion or indexing. (Earlier in the process, the House of Representatives proposed indexing effective after the year 2000 in its version of the 1997 tax act.) One great problem for indexing is that it creates far more complexity than exclusion: taxpayers would have to track each investment to establish its holding period. Ironically, the new tax law does the same thing without conveying any of the benefits of indexing, because the tax rate on capital gains depends on holding periods. Thus an economist might ask if indexing would be preferable to the current patchwork of tax preferences for capital gains. The political debate, however, centers on whether indexing would be a desirable addition to current law.

Would Indexing Enhance Economic Efficiency?

An ideal income tax would be neutral with respect to inflation. This means that taxes would take the same share of *real* income from capital—that is, income after removing the effects of inflation—no matter what happened to the general price level. In the case of capital gains, this would mean that if inflation caused the value of an asset to double over time, that fact by itself would have no bearing on how much tax was owed. Just as important, capital expense would also be indexed, so that if inflation caused interest expense to double in nominal terms, interest deductions would remain unchanged. Moreover, real capital gains would be taxed as they accrue, rather than only when realized.

Ignoring the high compliance costs that would accompany this "ideal" system, it would surely enhance economic efficiency. Most actual proposals for indexing have been far less comprehensive than the economist's ideal system, however, because they would not index other forms of capital income or capital expense. They would not tax gains on an accrual basis. And they would not even fully index capital gains and losses; gains would be indexed only to the extent that they exceeded inflation and losses would not be indexed at all. Although this last seems like a fine technical point, it probably vitiates whatever efficiency gains arise from indexing.

Pure Indexing versus Indexing with Asset Loss Limit

In principle, it would be straightforward to introduce indexing by simply replacing nominal realized capital gains with indexed (that is, real) capital gains. In the simplest case, a taxpayer would compute capital gain by multiplying the basis by a factor that reflects the increase in the price level since the asset was purchased. (The calculation would be more complicated for an asset that depreciates or is improved over time, as explained later in the chapter.) After adjusting the basis, all the calculations could proceed exactly as they do under current law.

But this straightforward approach would generate many more capital losses than exist under present law. Many long-held assets, especially those that have paid out income in the form of interest, rent, or dividends, are sold for a smaller real value than their purchase price, even though their nominal value has increased. And, of course, every asset sold at a nominal loss would have an even bigger loss after indexing. As table 6-9 showed, full indexing would have reduced the amount of taxable gains in 1993 by more than half, assuming that the overall $3,000 loss limit had been retained and taxpayer behavior was unaffected by the new rules.

Full indexing would thus entail a substantial revenue loss, and the losses would be even larger after behavioral responses are accounted for. Taxpayers who defer gains and realize losses (see chapter 4) would have a much greater chance of fully sheltering their gains from tax under full indexing because they would have more and bigger losses and smaller gains. To stem these revenue losses, proposals for indexing always limit the indexing adjustment to the amount of the nominal capital gain. Under this limit, an asset with a $10,000 nominal gain but a $10,000 real loss would be treated as having an indexed gain of 0. Assets with nominal losses would not be indexed at all.[1]

Indexing and Inflation

Pure indexing would make the real after-tax return to capital gains investments independent of the rate of inflation, assuming the indexing adjustment is approximately correct and that the $3,000 loss limit is not binding. In fact, there is no exact cost-of-living adjustment, so even pure indexing would correct only imperfectly for the effects of inflation. The consumer price index (CPI), which would be the likely instrument for indexation, overstates the effect of inflation, so indexing based on the CPI would cause real after-tax returns to be positively related to inflation and holding period.[2] In addition, the $3,000 loss limit is more likely to be binding at high inflation rates than at low ones. For this reason, even "pure" indexing might provide inadequate adjustment for inflation for some taxpayers. Since these two effects are relatively small and counterbalancing, pure indexing might provide a fairly good approximation for the effects of inflation.

Indexing with the asset-by-asset loss limit, however, would understate the effects of inflation, especially for risky and income-producing assets, because it treats gains and losses asymmetrically. It fully indexes gains only for those assets with real gains. For assets with nominal gains but real losses, indexing with a loss limit amounts to partial indexing. For assets with nominal losses, it does nothing at all.

Risky assets are by their nature more likely to produce losses than safe assets. Income-producing assets are more likely to be sold for less than their real purchase price because they pay out income rather than accrue it.

Indexing and Risk

Full indexing of assets for inflation significantly reduces the riskiness of investment in capital gains assets. It does this in two ways. First, it reduces the risk of unexpected inflation, a substantial risk for a long-term investment. Second, it reduces the variance of returns as compared with an exclusion or preferential tax rate designed to provide the same average amount of tax relief.[3]

The first point is obvious, but the second bears some explanation. For an asset held for a certain period of time—say ten years—indexing reduces the taxable gain by a fixed amount corresponding to the increase in the basis attributable to inflation. Beyond that fixed adjustment, any gain or loss is fully taxable. The government takes a portion of real gains and rebates the same portion of real losses. For an asset purchased for $1,000 and sold ten years later, over which period the price level had doubled, the excess of the sale price above $2,000—the adjusted basis—would be taxed fully and any shortfall would be fully deductible. If the asset sold for $5,000 and the tax rate was 40 percent, the tax under indexing would be $1,200 (40 percent of the $3,000 real gain). If it sold for $1,000, indexing would result in a tax *savings* of $400 (40 percent of a $1,000 real loss).

Although real before-tax returns range from –$1,000 to +$3,000, the after-tax range under indexing is reduced by 40 percent, to –$600 to +$1,800. This example illustrates how full indexing reduces the variance of returns.

If capital gains are instead taxed at a rate of 20 percent (either through an exclusion or a preferential tax rate on long-term gains), the range of returns is much bigger. If the asset is sold for $5,000, it earns a nominal gain of $4,000, yielding a tax bill of $800 (20 percent of $4,000). If it is sold for $1,000, there is no capital gains tax. The range of after-tax real returns is –$1,000 to $2,200. Thus even though the average tax is the same ($400) under both the exclusion and indexing, indexing reduces the range (variance) of returns by much more.

The reduction in variance is even greater ex ante when considering an investment, because inflation could turn out to be greater or smaller than the $1,000 that actually occurred. If inflation were higher, under the exclusion the capital gains tax would increase with inflation, whereas under indexing the tax would not change. Clearly, pure indexing would reduce risk much more than an exclusion that provided the same average tax savings.

Indexing with the loss limit has less desirable properties. In the example, the tax under indexing with loss limit would be the same as under the exclusion (zero) in a case where the asset declines in real value. The range of after-tax returns becomes –$1,000 to $2,800. Thus the loss limit increases the variation in after-tax returns. More important, the average tax bill goes up compared with pure indexing because of the asymmetric treatment of gains and losses. Since the loss limit only affects assets with real losses, which are most likely to occur for risky assets, it amounts to a surtax on risky investments. Thus even though pure indexing has very desirable risk reduction properties, indexing with a loss limit does not.

Indexing and Lock-In

Both a preferential tax rate and indexing reduce lock-in by reducing tax liability when people sell assets with accrued gains. They have different relative effects, however, on different margins of choice: whether to sell an asset or to hold it until death; whether to sell an asset and purchase another asset that will be sold later.[4]

If the choice is between selling an asset or holding it until death, the relevant tax price of a sale is the ratio of the capital gains tax to the sale price of the asset. The burden of the capital gains tax is largest for assets with a high ratio of nominal gain to sale price, namely, those with a long holding period or a high nominal pretax return. Indexing would exclude a relatively small percentage of the nominal gains produced by assets of this kind. Thus an exclusion that has the same average burden on all investments as indexing is more effective in reducing lock-in for assets that the taxpayer does not intend to resell.

If the taxpayer intends to make future transactions, however, there is an offsetting benefit from indexing that an exclusion does not provide. An asset with a large accumulated gain has a relatively low tax basis and is thus not well insulated against future inflation. Suppose that a taxpayer in the 40 percent bracket holds an asset with a current price of $1,000 and a basis of $100. Suppose further that the taxpayer expects to sell the asset in ten years, when the price level will be twice as high. If the taxpayer continues to hold the asset, indexing will double the basis to $200 and produce a total tax saving, relative to full taxation of the nominal gain, of $40 (40 percent of the additional $100 of deduction). If, instead, the taxpayer sells the asset today and reinvests the net proceeds, the basis in the new asset today will be $640 ($1,000 minus $360 tax on the real gain of $900). Future inflation would then increase the basis to $1,320. The taxpayer would be paying an additional tax of $360 but gaining a tax benefit of $448 (40 percent of the additional deduction of $1,120) in ten years. This offsetting future tax benefit lowers significantly the net tax price of selling an asset today under indexing. Under certain circumstances, this benefit of increasing the basis can do as much to reduce lock-in as an exclusion of the same average magnitude as indexing.[5]

Indexing is a less effective means of reducing lock-in, however, when accompanied by a binding limit on the deductibility of real losses. This is because indexing with loss limits would create a new form of lock-in for assets with nominal gains, but real losses. For these assets, the marginal tax rate on future gains would be zero, which would provide a powerful incentive to hold the asset.

Suppose a taxpayer had purchased an asset for $100, and the asset had increased in nominal value to $130 but the price level had risen in the same period by 50 percent. The asset would have a nominal gain of $30 but a real loss of $20. Because of the loss limit, the loss would not be deductible if the asset were sold today. If the asset were instead held and it increased in real value by $1, the real loss would be $19. Tax liability would be unchanged because the loss would still not be deductible. In this case, the marginal tax rate on the additional gain is 0.

These discontinuities could create serious distortions in decisions to sell or hold assets. Individuals would have an additional incentive to avoid investing in assets that might produce real losses because losses would not be deductible. Once an individual had such an asset, however, he or she would have a strong incentive to continue to hold it. The asset would be like a tax-exempt bond, though only in the hands of the current investor. A powerful lock-in effect would occur because marginal gains would be taxed at a zero rate as long as the asset had a cumulative real loss.

Indexing and Tax Shelters

The biggest misconception about indexing is that it somehow avoids the incentives to create tax shelters that exist under an exclusion or preferential tax rate. That is simply not true. The motivation for tax shelters, as explained in chapter 5, is the difference between the taxation of capital gains and the taxation of other forms of interest and expense. Indexing exacerbates those differences.

If one can borrow and fully deduct the interest to invest in an asset whose real, but not nominal, return would be taxed, one can make money after tax even if the asset earns a below-market rate of return. The calculation is exactly the same as applies in the case of a preferential tax rate.[6]

Indexing and Fairness

Some argue that indexing capital gains for inflation is a simple matter of fairness, indeed, that not doing so is a "crime" and a "moral outrage."[7] This argument can be refuted on several grounds. First, anyone making an investment knows beforehand that nominal gains—not real gains—are subject to taxation. They will only make investments where the expected return net of expected taxes exceeds the net after-tax return from alternative investments, and the expected tax includes the tax on purely inflationary gains. Taxing inflationary gains might be undesirable, but it is not unfair ex ante because investors know about it before they make their investment decisions.

Second, even if fairness is assessed on an ex post basis, the argument for indexing capital gains alone is tenuous. As explained earlier, the inflation tax on bonds and other kinds of income-producing assets is greater than it is on capital gains assets, because tax cannot be deferred on non–capital gains assets. Indexing capital gains would exacerbate that difference, increasing the ex post horizontal inequity from unanticipated inflation.

Full indexing would improve equity among capital gains investments. When nominal gains are taxed, the real effective tax rate on different assets with the same real return varies with the holding period. If the nominal rate of return is 8 percent and the inflation rate is a constant 4 percent, an asset held five years faces an effective tax rate of 35.4 percent (assuming a 20 percent statutory rate), which is 12.4 percentage points higher than the effective rate on a similar asset held twenty years (23 percent). If the basis is indexed before calculating the gain, the difference in effective tax rates falls to less than 4 percentage points (18.8 percent for the five-year holding period compared with 15.1 percent for the twenty-year holding period).

If there is an argument for indexing on equity grounds, it is that the benefits are more progressively distributed under indexing than under a maximum rate or partial exclusion. In 1993 the average sale of corporate stock would have produced a real capital loss after indexation for taxpayers with incomes of less than $50,000 (see table 6-10). In contrast, nearly half of capital gains on stock realized by people with an income of $200,000 or more was real. If losses were limited as under current law, the nominal gain of $25 billion realized by people with the highest income would correspond to a $21 billion indexed gain; that is, only 14 percent of their gain would be excluded under indexation. In contrast, the $14 billion in nominal gains realized by everyone else would translate into $5 billion in taxable income; 61 percent would be excluded.

The asset-by-asset loss limitation would reduce the benefits of indexing in every income class. It appears, however, that such a loss limit would have slightly greater effect on higher-income taxpayers than those with lower incomes.[8] Lower-income people are hurt by the indexing loss limit because they are more likely to have real losses, but higher-income people lose out because they are more likely to have sold many assets, some with real gains and others with real losses. Data from 1985 suggest that the latter effect may be more significant.[9]

Complications under Indexing

As already mentioned, indexing capital gains for inflation would significantly complicate the tax system. Current law will eventually require taxpayers to calculate gain for assets in four holding-period classes, a prospect that has caused much complaint among taxpayers. Indexing would in effect create a separate holding-period class for every quarter year. For example, an investor who sells shares in a mutual fund held for ten years in which quarterly dividends were reinvested might have to make forty indexing calculations to calculate taxable gain.[10] If shares had been purchased periodically over the ten-year period, even more calculations could be necessary. Mutual fund companies could help investors by calculating an indexed average basis on sales of shares but may be reluctant to do this.[11]

Indexing would require extensive calculations for an asset that is improved over time, such as an apartment building or a business. Every improvement would have to be treated as a separate asset with a separate indexing adjustment. Many indexing proposals apply to only certain classes of assets, in an effort to limit revenue losses and tax-shelter possibilities, but this means that some of the components of a business or other improved property might qualify for indexing, whereas others might not—another complexity.

The worst case for complexity would apply to the shareholder of an intermediary, such as a partnership, that held a mix of assets, only some of which qualified for indexing.[12] The partnership would have to allocate the tax basis between qualifying and nonqualifying components. Each of the qualifying components would have to be indexed separately on the basis of its holding period. Allocation could be extremely complex for an intermediary that bought and sold frequently. Both taxpayers and the IRS would have to trace qualifying and nonqualifying indexed bases through multiple layers of partnerships (partnership 1 owning partnership 2, which owns partnership 3, and so forth). The Treasury would probably have to write complex regulations to prevent deliberate abuse, but these regulations would also make compliance more difficult for many taxpayers holding shares in limited partnerships.[13]

8

ALTERNATIVE WAYS OF TAXING CAPITAL GAINS

The complex web of preferential rates for capital gains enacted in 1997 represented a significant change in the way capital gains are taxed, but there are many other options. Many people expected Congress to reintroduce a partial exclusion for capital gains, as had been in effect before 1987. An exclusion would have been simpler and would have given everyone who realizes a long-term capital gain the same proportional reduction in capital gains tax. In contrast, the 20 percent maximum rate excludes nearly half of capital gains for taxpayers in the 39.6 percent bracket, but less than 30 percent for taxpayers in the 28 percent bracket.

Indexing capital gains for inflation, discussed in the previous chapter, would have been more complex but would have provided somewhat more benefits to lower-income investors and also some protection against the effects of inflation. Fundamental tax reform, in the form of a flat tax or other form of consumption tax, would virtually end the taxation of capital gains at the individual level.

This chapter examines options to change the taxation of capital gains other than indexation, starting with fundamental tax reform and then turning to incremental options. Chapter 9 lays out some options for change that are better targeted at the objectives of capital gains tax relief than the approaches chosen so far.

Capital Gains and Fundamental Tax Reform

Some tax reform options that are being debated would fundamentally change the way capital gains are taxed. Under a consumption tax, such as a value added tax or the Hall-Rabushka flat tax, capital income is untaxed. Capital gains, per se, would not be explicitly included in the tax base. Ending the tax on capital gains as part of fundamental tax reform would avoid many of the problems inherent in providing a tax preference solely for capital gains. Because other forms of capital income would also be untaxed and interest expense would not be deductible, the incentive to create tax shelters to convert ordinary income into capital gains, or to borrow with fully deductible interest to earn tax-preferred capital gains, would be diminished substantially. (There could still be an incentive under the flat tax and other income-based consumption tax proposals to try to recharacterize wages as capital gains.)

As a solution to the many difficulties outlined earlier, giving up trying to tax capital income at all would be decidedly extreme and unfair, since the primary beneficiaries would be those most able to pay tax. Other, less publicized reforms would significantly change the tax treatment of capital gains without giving up on taxing capital income altogether. A pure comprehensive income tax would measure real (inflation-adjusted) income on an accrual basis. That is, capital gains would be taxed as they accrued, rather than when assets were sold, but only the gain in excess of inflation would be subject to tax. Under such a definition of income, interest income and expense would also be measured in real terms. Full indexation of the income tax with accrual taxation would remove most opportunities for tax shelters that are created by differences in the taxation of income and expense. It would end lock-in because taxes are assessed on accrued gains annually, whether or not assets are sold. Thus one could not avoid or defer tax by holding onto an asset.

Under an ideal income tax, corporations would not be subject to a separate level of taxation, as they are now. Rather, corporate tax liability would be integrated with the individual income tax. Corporate income would be taxable to individuals as it accrues, and sales of corporate stock would not be subject to additional tax.[1] Corporations would be treated the same way as small unincorporated businesses.

The major drawback of the ideal income tax, however, is that it would make measuring income much more complex for many taxpayers. Accrual taxation would require the annual assessment of asset values—not a great burden for publicly traded assets, but a very costly proposition for assets such as buildings, businesses, and works of art.

Design Issues

Short of fundamental tax reform, capital gains could be taxed in many different ways under the income tax. A tax cut could assume the form of a maximum tax rate below the top statutory rate (as under present law), a partial exclusion, indexing, or some combination. The tax base that qualifies for the cut raises additional questions. Which gains should qualify for the preferential tax status? Should the tax rate vary by holding period or by type of asset? Should the tax apply to all capital gains, only to capital gains that occur after an effective date, or only to capital gains on assets purchased after the effective date?

Fixed Exclusion

Under a fixed exclusion, a portion of capital gains is excluded from taxable income. Before 1987, 60 percent of long-term capital gains were excluded from taxable income. Thus a taxpayer in the ordinary income top bracket at that time—50 percent—paid an effective rate on capital gains of 20 percent (50 percent reduced by the 60 percent exclusion).

An exclusion is simpler to administer and comply with than are maximum tax rates. Taxpayers would include a fraction of their long-term capital gains in income, rather than the entire amount, and would not need to do a separate maximum tax rate calculation (or several as under current law). An exclusion also provides the same percentage reduction in capital gains tax rates to everybody. The maximum tax rate provides the greatest benefit to taxpayers in the top bracket.

Table 8-1. Effective Long-Term Capital Gains Tax Rates under 40 Percent Exclusion Compared with Present Law

Percent

Ordinary income tax bracket	Current long-term gains rate[a]	Effective rate after 40 percent exclusion
15.0	10.0	9.0
28.0	20.0	16.8
31.0	20.0	18.6
36.0	20.0	21.6
39.6	20.0	23.8

a. Rate applying to gains held one to four years.

To illustrate, table 8-1 compares the effective tax rates on capital gains under a 40 percent exclusion with the rates that apply to gains held more than one year under current law. Taxpayers in the top two brackets (applying to incomes of $163,950 or more for couples in 1997) would pay slightly higher rates. The 98 percent or more of taxpayers in the other three tax brackets would face lower rates on capital gains than under present law.[2]

Nonetheless, significant complexities remain under an exclusion. Taxpayers still must segregate short-term from long-term capital gains—as they do at present—and losses are subject to a separate limit in each category. Losses that cannot be used currently must be tracked separately and carried over. The difference in rates between short- and long-term capital gains creates incentives to manipulate the timing of gains and losses, especially by realizing losses when they qualify for the higher short-term rates and deferring gains until they qualify for the exclusion. But these complexities exist under the current regime, and many others would be avoided with a flat exclusion.

Variable Exclusion

Under a variable exclusion, the portion of capital gains included in taxable income varies with the length of time an asset is held. The Bush administration's 1992 budget proposed an exclusion that would range from 15 percent for assets held at least one year up to 45 percent for assets held at least three years. A variable exclusion applied in the 1930s. (Note that the flat exclusion for long-term capital gains in effect before 1987 was in essence a variable exclusion, but with only two exclusion percentages, 0 and 60 percent.)

The current system of maximum tax rates also varies with the holding period. The rates of 20 percent and 18 percent for assets held by high-bracket investors for successively longer periods might be replaced with increasing exclusion rates. For example, exclusion rates of 44 percent and 50 percent would produce the same effective tax rates for a taxpayer in the 36 percent ordinary income tax bracket. The graduated exclusion would retain the progressivity with tax rates without the cumbersome addition of two sets of maximum rates under present law.

Nonetheless, a system of graduated exclusions is more complicated than a single flat exclusion. Moreover, there is no clear policy rationale for capital gains tax rates that decline with the holding period, however implemented. Even without any rate preference, the effective tax rate on capital gains declines with the holding period because of the benefit of deferral (see chapter 4). This decline in effective tax rates is an aspect of the lock-in effect that concerns critics of capital gains taxation. Creating capital gains tax rates that decline with holding periods exacerbates lock-in for assets with gains until the minimum tax rate is achieved.

Also, even if the policy objective is to encourage investors to be patient, a schedule of tax rates that declines with holding periods might be counterproductive. Presumably, policymakers would like to encourage investors with losses to hold onto their assets as much as they want to encourage investors with gains, but the falling rates have exactly the opposite effect.[3] Taxpayers have an incentive to accelerate the realization of short-term losses before they qualify for long-term status, because a dollar of short-term losses on an asset held eleven months, say, can save up to 39.6¢ in taxes, compared with 20¢ or less if held for twelve months or more. Clearly, some investors will realize short-term losses even if they are bullish on the asset's long-term prospects.

Progressive Rates

Compared with full taxation of capital gains, the set of maximum tax rates on capital gains under current law provides the largest benefits to people with high incomes, but capital gains tax relief may be targeted at people with lower incomes. In 1992 the Congress passed a tax cut on capital gains realized by people with lower incomes as part of a broader bill that President George Bush vetoed. It would have had little or no effect on those taxpayers who realize most of the capital gains, but would have given relief to taxpayers who realize gains only infrequently.

Another way to achieve progressivity is to exclude a certain dollar amount of capital gains from tax each year. If gains of less than $10,000 had been exempt from tax in 1993, the number of returns with capital gains would have fallen by 72 percent, but only about 30 percent of capital gains would have been excluded from tax.[4] This option would vastly simplify accounting for capital gains for the majority of investors. Its disadvantage is that it would probably have been scored as a revenue loser compared with the change brought by the Tax Reform Act of 1997, because there would not be any feedback effect on taxable realizations. Taxpayers who realized more than $10,000 in gains would have no tax incentive to sell more assets, and taxpayers who realized less than $10,000 would not be taxed on their realizations, so their behavioral response does not create additional tax revenues. Note that such an exclusion was enacted for owner-occupied housing as part of the Taxpayer Relief Act of 1997 (see chapter 2).

Lifetime Exclusion

Another option would allow taxpayers to realize a limited amount of capital gains tax-free over the course of their lives. Canada takes that approach, which exempts almost all Canadians from capital gains taxation. The drawback is that it complicates enforcement and compliance because the unused portion of the lifetime exclusion would have to be carried over from year to year. Like the progressive rate option, a lifetime exclusion would have little or no effect on the decisions of taxpayers who realize the most capital gains.

Rollover of Gain

Another option discussed during the debate leading up to the 1997 tax act was expanded rollover treatment for capital gains assets. Under current law, investors who exchange property for similar property can defer realization of gains (see chapter 2). Like-kind exchanges generally apply to real estate, although taxpayers are often allowed to defer realizing a gain when their stock in a company is replaced by the stock of an acquiring company, and homeowners were allowed to roll over the gain on most home sales until 1997. The 1997 law also allows rollover when the proceeds from the sale of shares in one qualifying small business are reinvested in another qualifying small business.

Like-kind exchange treatment could be extended to other assets when the proceeds from a sale are reinvested in another similar asset. Suppose an investor sold 100 shares of company X and reinvested the proceeds in company Z; the new asset could acquire the basis of the old asset and no gain would be recognized until shares in Z (or a subsequent stock on the rollover chain) are sold.

Advocates of this approach argue that the tax code should distinguish between sales of assets to finance consumption and sales in which the proceeds are reinvested. It might also be argued that this option is a natural extension of the realization principle of taxation: that is, tax is due only when the owner of an asset has exchanged it for cash.

On the other hand, taxing gains only upon realization is the source of most of the problems in taxing capital gains. Expanding the scope of deferral would compound these problems. In combination with the nontaxation of capital gains at death, unlimited rollovers would make it easier for wealthy investors to avoid paying tax on capital gains entirely but would do little or nothing for small investors. Investors with a single asset may be reticent to buy another similar asset with the proceeds of the sale, especially if they wanted to finance their retirement with the proceeds of the sale. In contrast, wealthy, well-diversified investors could sell assets with losses or small gains to finance consumption, while rolling over the proceeds of sales of assets with gains.

Rollover treatment could make accounting for gains from mutual funds easier, because gains tax would be due only upon sale, but it would make accounting for other rollover assets more complicated. An asset's cost basis could be an amalgam of the bases of many different assets purchased over many years and rolled over. It would be difficult for the IRS to administer such a provision.

A large factor in the decision to replace the rollover provision for owner-occupied housing with an exclusion was the fact that it was extremely complex and difficult to enforce at the same time that it collected little tax revenue.[5] In economic terms, the rollover provision resulted in a large deadweight loss compared with its revenue yield and was thus a very inefficient tax.[6] A broader rollover provision would have many of the same drawbacks.[7]

Retrospective Taxation

As mentioned at the outset, many problems arise because capital gains cannot be taxed on an accrual basis, certainly for political reasons, and probably for practical reasons as well. Of the alternative methods that do not require annual valuations, one is functionally equivalent to accrual, as it would require an annual deposit of tax on account for every asset held with a final reckoning upon sale that takes account of the advantage of deferral.[8] This approach is only neutral with respect to holding period if the tax authority can determine the actual time path of capital gains, a source of great complexity for publicly traded assets such as corporate stock and an impossibility for other kinds of assets.[9] Moreover, the method violates the realization principle, as tax is due in advance of a realization.

Another proposed alternative, which is based entirely upon sale price, is neutral with respect to holding period—that is, it does not create lock-in—as long as assets are taxed at death.[10] Rather than taxing the actual gain or loss, "retrospective capital gains taxation" would impute a normal gain given a risk-free rate of return (which may vary over time) and the holding period. If the risk-free rate of return is a constant 6 percent and an asset sold for $10,000 after being held for ten years, the imputed capital gain would be $4,416.[11] Absent taxes, an investor will hold assets that, after adjusting for risk, are expected to pay at least the risk-free rate of return and will sell assets that are expected to pay less. Retrospective taxation does not alter these incentives and is thus neutral with respect to holding period. Put another way, this proposal would end lock-in.

The practical problem with this approach is that it depends solely on the sale price of an asset. The asset sold for $10,000 might have been purchased for $100,000, but it would still have a taxable "gain." Conversely, someone who realizes $10,000 from the sale of Microsoft stock purchased five years ago (33 percent annual rate of return) would have the same taxable gain as someone who realized $10,000 from the sale of stock in Crown Books (currently in Chapter 11) purchased at the same time. Although undeniably economically efficient and fair ex ante, it would be hard to convince any politician of the fairness of this approach.

Tax Capital Gains at Death

The failure to tax capital gains that are held until death is a major factor in the lock-in effect. Taxing capital gains at death would go a long way toward removing the lock-in effect. Taxpayers could still defer capital gains tax liability by avoiding asset sales, but they could no longer avoid it entirely by holding assets until death. It would increase tax revenues both directly from the tax collected on a decedent's income tax returns and indirectly by inducing more realizations of capital gains during life.

Taxing gains at death would enhance economic efficiency by deterring expensive tax-avoidance schemes. It would make the tax system fairer because these devices are mainly feasible only for wealthy people with very large capital gains. Taxing capital gains at death would have the disadvantage of causing some heirs to sell assets to pay their tax liability, even if they wanted to continue holding them. This would raise especially strong concerns in the case of a family farm or business. For this reason, small family farms or businesses could be exempt from the capital gains tax at death.[12]

An alternative approach that addresses the cash-flow concerns is to enact a carryover basis provision, so the heirs of appreciated property do not pay the accrued capital gains tax liability until they sell the asset. Carryover basis is the rule for assets that are transferred as gifts during life and was actually enacted into law in 1976, although it was repealed before it could take effect (see chapter 2). Enacting carryover basis would remove the disincentive for parents to transfer assets to their children while they are still alive. Taxing capital gains at death would actually give donors a positive incentive to make transfers during life compared with holding until death, since recipients of gifts can continue to defer realization of capital gain.

Either approach would create complexity. If capital gains were taxed at death, the executor of the estate would need information about the basis of assets held, which might not be easily assembled. Calculating basis would be especially daunting for an asset that had been improved or modified over time, such as a business. A carryover basis rule would obviate the need to calculate gain at death, but the challenge of reconstructing basis for an asset that had been transferred between several generations would be even more difficult.

One way to deal with these concerns would be to allow taxpayers to deem a basis equal to some percentage of the value of an asset at death. As one possibility, taxpayers could assume that their basis was 50 percent of the value of the asset at death without providing any documentation. This would reduce the tax on all assets with gains greater than 50 percent of value—and primarily benefit long-held assets and particularly successful investments—but, compared with current law, it would still reduce the incentive to hold assets until death.

Eligibility of Assets

The debate about whether to cut taxes on capital gains has generally focused on a permanent reduction in the tax rate for any qualifying asset, regardless of when the asset was purchased. But a reduction in taxes on capital gains does not have to be carried out in that way. It could apply to all capital gains on all assets, but only temporarily. It could be permanent, but limited to capital gains on assets purchased after a certain date. A cut in the tax rate on capital gains could also combine these features.

For example, the Balanced Budget Act of 1995 would have combined an immediate exclusion for all capital gains with indexing only for certain assets purchased after 2000. The act would have limited indexing to new assets in order to reduce the revenue cost. In fact, because people would have an incentive to realize capital gains immediately in order to qualify for indexing on future inflation, the indexing portion of the act actually would have raised revenues in the short run. Indeed, the eligibility rules for a new tax preference can have important effects on tax revenues in the short run. They also have implications for economic efficiency (also in the short run).[13]

Options for Determining Eligibility of Assets

Some proposals would provide tax relief only to those who have capital gains from certain kinds of assets, or assets purchased after a certain date. Many indexing proposals, for example, would only apply to assets purchased after a certain date, such as the date a law was enacted. The 18 percent rate on assets held for five or more years enacted as part of TRA97 is such a prospective provision. A prospective tax cut would ascribe no direct benefit to assets that had been purchased before the effective date, but over time would cover all asset sales. A prospective tax cut would provide exactly the same incentives for new investment as a tax cut that applied to all sales but would have a smaller revenue cost.

Some past proposals, such as the one advanced by Representatives Ed Jenkins, Bill Archer, and Ronnie G. Flippo in 1989, would have provided a capital gains tax preference for only a fixed period of time, after which the preference was either to expire or be replaced by a prospective tax reduction. Although it is not uncommon for tax legislation to carry an expiration date—in order to limit revenue losses or to allow reevaluation of the benefits and costs of the legislation—there has never been a temporary capital gains tax cut.

How Eligibility Affects Revenues

A tax cut that applied to all sales—a retrospective tax cut—encourages sales by lowering the cost of selling assets. A prospective tax cut also encourages sales, but by raising the after-tax rate of return on new investments in relation to assets in the portfolio. That is because the prospective tax cut applies only to new investments.

Because new investments would be taxed less than old ones under a prospective tax cut, taxpayers have an incentive to sell old assets and buy new ones. They may also choose to "mark to market" old assets, that is, pay tax on the accumulated capital gain so that any future capital gain qualifies for the preferential tax treatment. (Mark-to-market is equivalent, for tax purposes, to selling the asset and buying back an identical one.)

A prospective tax cut motivates investors to sell assets but avoids cutting taxes on assets that would have been sold even if the tax law were not changed. In the short run, any induced sales of old assets are taxed at full rates under a prospective tax reduction, as opposed to the reduced rates under a retrospective cut.

A prospective tax cut is likely to gain more revenue in the short run than a retrospective cut. Suppose that without a change in tax law, capital gains realizations are $150 billion and taxed at an average rate of 25 percent. Baseline revenues would be $37.5 billion. Suppose that cutting the tax rate in half—to 12.5 percent—would cause realizations to double in the short run (to $300 billion). The revenue cost of the retrospective tax cut would be zero. That is, the increased realizations would offset the exclusion. (Realizations of $300 billion taxed at 12.5 percent produce the same amount of revenue as $150 billion of realizations taxed at 25 percent.)

If the tax cut were prospective, however, and the same amount of realizations were induced in the short run, revenues would double. The doubling takes place because all of the induced realizations, as well as all of the realizations that would have occurred in the absence of a tax cut, would be fully taxed at the 25 percent rate. That is, $300 billion worth of realizations taxed at 25 percent produces revenues of $75 billion, twice the baseline revenues. Thus, even if the realizations induced under the prospective tax cut were much smaller than under the retrospective change, the revenue effect would be positive. If realizations increased by just 10 percent, or $15 billion, revenue would also increase by 10 percent, or $3.75 billion. Therefore, despite many fewer induced realizations, the prospective cut would still produce more revenue in the short run than the retrospective tax cut.

Over a sufficiently long period, prospective and retrospective tax cuts have identical effects because all assets eventually qualify for the prospective tax cut. Despite the long-run equivalence, part of the short-run revenue gain under the prospective cut is a permanent revenue gain. Revenue losses do not offset the short-run revenue gain over the long term. The reason is that the prospective tax cut does not provide any direct tax benefits for assets that were purchased before the enacting legislation's effective date. Note, however, that the part of the revenue gain caused by mark-to-market is not permanent, but only a shift in the timing of realizations. The sale of assets is accelerated to shelter future gains.

Some proposals for a capital gains cut have called for indexing the cost basis to offset the effects of inflation rather than directly reducing the tax rate through an exclusion. Since inflation is a substantial part of most capital gains, indexing offers a tax benefit equivalent to a substantial exclusion. Prospective indexing, which would apply only to newly purchased assets, would also provide a stronger incentive than would a retrospective tax reduction to sell assets in the short run. Another variation of indexing, which would index all assets (new and old) for future inflation, affords an incentive to sell assets that is similar to that provided by a retrospective exclusion.

Temporary exclusion followed by prospective indexing is another option. The temporary exclusion applies to old assets (that is, retrospectively) as well as new ones. This option provides a very strong incentive to sell assets, stronger, in fact, than the incentive that existed at the end of 1986, when capital gains realizations doubled in anticipation of the higher tax rates that would take effect with the Tax Reform Act of 1986.[14]

Although a temporary tax cut would prompt a large number of realizations, it is uncertain whether such a cut would raise more or less revenue than a prospective tax cut. The reason for the uncertainty is that the temporary tax cut must stimulate enough new realizations to offset the revenue lost on sales that would have occurred without a tax cut (sometimes called the static revenue loss). But the short-term revenues under either a temporary or retrospective tax cut are at the expense of future tax revenues. Furthermore, in the case of the temporary tax cut, this acceleration of revenues is unfavorable to the government. The government loses more in future revenues, when discounted back to the present, than it gains in the near term.

Patterns of Revenue in the Long and Short Run

The effect of a reduction of capital gains taxes on revenues depends on the parameters of the proposal—for instance, the percentage excluded and whether it applies to old assets or just newly purchased ones—and how taxpayers respond to the changed incentives. If taxpayers' behavior did not change at all, if the 28 percent maximum tax rate had been replaced with a 50 percent exclusion in 1997, say, average tax rates and tax revenues from long-term gains would have fallen by about 35 percent. As explained earlier, however, taxpayers would realize more capital gains if the tax rate was lower; therefore, a portion of the "static" revenue loss—that is, before considering how taxpayers' behavior changes—would be offset by the induced realizations.[15] In addition, if taxpayers convert other income that would have been fully taxed into capital gains, the behavioral response causes a partly offsetting revenue loss. In the short term, a 50 percent exclusion, effective January 1, 1997, would have increased tax revenues because of a short-term "unlocking effect." Taxpayers may sell assets that they have been holding simply because of the higher tax rates.

As a result, the Joint Committee on Taxation estimated that a 50 percent exclusion would raise $3 billion in tax revenues in fiscal

1997 and 1998, the latter being the first full year for which the proposal would be in effect. After that, the exclusion would cause a net loss of revenues, growing from $3 billion in 1999 to $12 billion in 2006. The revenue loss is more than three times as large in the second five years as in the first five. Between 1997 and 2001, the exclusion would reduce federal income tax revenues by $14 billion. Between 2002 and 2006, revenues would fall by $49 billion.

The revenue loss from prospectively indexing capital gains for inflation on corporate stock and tangible business property, such as buildings and equipment, would have been even more skewed. As under an exclusion, revenues would have increased in the short run, but for a different reason. Taxpayers would have been permitted to mark to market assets in the first year so that they would be indexed for inflation in the future. This mark-to-market causes revenues to increase by $1 billion in the first two years. After that, the proposed indexing would lose revenue, and the losses would increase rapidly as the portion of capital gains indexed for inflation accumulated over time. Between 1997 and 2001, prospective indexing would cost only $2 billion. Between 2002 and 2006, it would cost ten times as much, about $21 billion. Even in 2006, the revenue loss would grow more rapidly under indexing than under the exclusion, as a larger percentage of gains would qualify for indexation. In the long run, indexation would cost less than a 50 percent exclusion because it would apply only to selected assets and inflation is expected to be moderate. But the difference in revenue loss is vastly overstated by the difference in short-term revenues.

BEYOND CAVEMAN
TAX POLICY

One of the characters on NBC's satirical television program, *Saturday Night Live*, was Unfrozen Caveman Lawyer. After having been frozen for aeons, he was thawed by scientists in time to embark on a successful legal career. When he decided to run for the Senate, he allowed as how he was confused and frightened by modern society and did not understand much, but the one thing that he did know for certain was that the tax rate on capital gains must be lowered.

"Caveman lawyer" was a parody of politicians who view capital gains tax cuts as a simple panacea. The parody was right on the mark in noting that cutting capital gains taxes has become a surefire applause line for some audiences, but few of the advocates of lower rates seem to understand the trade-offs involved.

Response to the Arguments
for Capital Gains Tax Preference

Little of the argument for a significant differential between ordinary income and capital gains tax rates, described in chapter 1, withstands close scrutiny. The tax preference for capital gains is unfair and highly complex. Although the tax incentives for capital gains might, on net, increase personal saving slightly, they reduce public saving more. Moreover, the current system wastes society's scarce resources by encouraging inefficient tax shelters and distorting the nature of investment.

Tax preferences are more likely to depress economic productivity than to improve it. A tax preference for capital gains might actually increase personal saving, although this is by no means assured. As a practical matter, capital gains earned by individuals subject to the individual income tax are a small fraction of the returns from saving. Thus subsidizing capital gains has little effect on the overall incentive to save. If anything, incentives to save may perversely discourage saving by making it possible for people to save less but still achieve their target levels of future consumption.

As for its effect on revenues, a capital gains preference almost surely reduces tax revenues. Careful econometric studies find that capital gains are relatively unresponsive to statutory changes in tax rates, even though the timing of gains is highly sensitive to year-to-year variations in rates. Equally important, a large difference between the rates on capital gains and other income gives taxpayers a strong incentive to convert other income into capital gains. The reduction in other income, which would otherwise be taxed at higher rates, produces a revenue loss to the government not measured in the empirical studies of capital gains.

A capital gains tax preference probably does reduce lock-in, but it is not clear that this is very important. The current system of rates, which declines with the holding period of capital assets, is counterproductive if lock-in is a serious concern.

A capital gains tax preference does reduce the overall tax burden on investments in corporate stock, offsetting part of the corporate income tax, but it is a crude instrument for doing so. It might not even increase the demand for corporate stock because the same preference applies to all forms of capital gains assets, not just stock.

The effects on risk-taking and entrepreneurship are ambiguous, but almost surely small. The tax on capital gains amounts to a risk-sharing arrangement between the government and investors, albeit at a price, and thus might actually encourage risk-taking. Most entrepreneurial capital comes from sources unaffected by the personal tax on capital gains. Thus personal income tax cuts are an ineffective way to stimulate venture capital.

Capital gains preferences hamper the economy primarily by prodding taxpayers to artificially convert other income into capital gains. Aside from costing the government revenues and raising questions about the fairness of the tax system, such conversions are wasteful. Talented people spend their time trying to figure out how to convert other income into capital gains instead of doing something socially productive. Moreover, because capital gains are taxed less heavily than other forms of income from capital, people have an incentive to make investments that produce capital gains, even if they pay lower rates of return than other less-favored investments. This is inefficient.

Taxing capital gains like other income is the fairest option. A rate preference for capital gains provides an unfair advantage to people who can earn a large share of their income in that form. That is, it favors the wealthy over others, and those with a great deal of flexibility about how to receive their income over those who have little choice but to take their income in a more heavily taxed form, such as wages and interest.

It is true that people who realize an isolated capital gain may look much better off in the year they realize the gain than they really are. But this is a flaw with a tax system based on realization, not a flaw with taxing capital gains per se. In fact, the same persons look less well off in each year that they defer realizing a capital gain, because some of their income is unreported on a tax form. On balance, the notion that capital gains are primarily the provenance of the rich is accurate, even when data are examined over many years.

It might be undesirable to tax income solely attributable to inflation, but it is not unfair to tax nominal capital gains in the context of the present system. The inflation tax on capital gains would actually be smaller than the tax on other kinds of capital income such as interest and dividends, even without preferential tax rates, because capital gains can be deferred, whereas other forms of capital income are taxed as they are earned. Thus adjusting capital gains for inflation would provide an unfair advantage for capital gains assets over other forms of assets and would increase the incentive to convert other income into capital gains.

The nation's trading partners tend to tax capital gains at lower rates. This is true, but it is unclear how it is relevant. The nation's major trading partners also tend to have much larger governments and socialized medicine, but the advocates of tax subsidies for capital gains would presumably not adopt these features in order to enhance America's international competitiveness. My guess is that when tax-payers become as adept at converting other income into capital gains in those countries as they are in the United States, its trading partners will be looking to the United States as a model for tax reform.

New Directions for Capital Gains Tax Policy

A friend of mine has earned the nickname Don Quixote because he worked on the abortive effort to repeal step-up in basis in the late 1970s and still thinks it was a good idea. I do, too, but it is obvious that the political currents are headed in the opposite direction. Many in Congress would like to cut the tax rate on capital gains further, to 15 percent or less. Representative Bill Archer, chairman of the House Committee on Ways and Means, which originates all tax legislation, has long been committed to indexing capital gains for inflation.

Either of these changes would be a mistake. A 15 percent tax rate on capital gains would give top-bracket taxpayers a huge incentive to convert other income into capital gains, exacerbating the inefficiency of the present system. Since realizations of capital gains are more sensitive at high tax rates than at low ones, the revenue cost of cutting rates from 20 percent to 15 percent would probably be much larger than the cost of the last rate reduction (from 28 percent to 20 percent). And, of course, it would provide a windfall to the rich.

Indexing would make the taxation of capital gains still more complex and would not make the tax system any more neutral with respect to inflation, as explained in chapter 7. Like the rate cut, indexing would create a significant incentive to convert income in other forms into capital gains and to invest in unproductive tax shelters.

Short of attacking windmills with Don Quixote, some things could be done in the short run to simplify the taxation of capital gains and make it fairer. The current taxation of capital gains is needlessly complex, even if one accepts the premise that capital gains should be taxed at lower rates than other income. Reducing tax rates with the holding period does not even approximately adjust for the effects of inflation: the inflation tax declines with holding period, all else being equal. Nor does it encourage investors to be patient. Although it encourages them to hold assets with gains, it also encourages the sale of assets with losses.

Thus, at a minimum, there should be fewer holding-period classes. Congress made a move toward this end in 1998 by ending the twelve- to eighteen-month category. It should also end the five-year holding category before people have marked assets to market in 2001 and thus feel entitled to the 18 percent tax rate scheduled to take effect for assets purchased or marked to market after 2000 and held five years. If they fail to do this, the Schedule D form (shown in appendix A) will no longer fit on two pages.

That approach is the next best thing—in terms of simplicity—to taxing capital gains in full. Taxable long-term capital gains would simply be defined to be a set percentage of realized long-term capital gains. Instead of having numerous classes of assets that are taxed at different rates, gains on all assets should be subject to the same exclusion, as they were before 1987. For reasons of both simplicity and efficiency, real estate should be treated the same as other depreciable assets.

A quick look at the Schedule D in appendix A makes clear how significant a simplification this would be. Replacing the maximum tax rate with an exclusion would render part IV—most of page 2— irrelevant. In net, the two-page tax form could be reduced to little more than a page. Moreover, the maximum tax rate calculations under the alternative minimum tax would be unnecessary, removing page 2 from the tax schedule used to compute that liability.

A flat exclusion would also be fairer, as explained in chapter 7. Assuming that the current tax rate structure could be replaced by a flat 30 percent exclusion on a revenue-neutral basis, taxpayers in the bottom tax brackets would pay effective capital gains tax rates on long-term gains that are close to what they pay now. Taxpayers in higher tax brackets would face higher tax rates on their long-term capital gains. The top tax rate on capital gains would be about equal to the 28 percent top rate on long-term capital gains in effect before 1997.

That approach has the advantage of taxing capital gains more like other forms of income, without the obvious political disadvantage of raising the overall tax burden on capital gains. It would reduce the incentive for high-income people to invest in tax shelters or to recharacterize income from wages or other fully taxed forms as capital gains. (If the exclusion is larger than 30 percent, people with lower incomes would have more incentive to convert ordinary income to capital gains, but they would be less able to do it.)

In the long run, fundamental reform is probably necessary because the distinction between capital gains and other income has become increasingly difficult to enforce in a fair and comprehensible way. One way to deal with this problem would be to remove the distinction, as was done half-heartedly in 1986.[1]

The 1986 act would be a good model for reform. Its avowed purpose was to promote "fairness, simplicity, and economic growth."[2] Although many question whether the Tax Reform Act of 1986 advanced the goal of simplicity, the treatment of capital gains after 1986 was a major simplification, but one only partly realized. Taxing capital gains and other income at the same rate means that, except for the necessary limits on losses (explained in chapter 2), capital gains are no more complicated than interest and dividends. Of course, the *next* TRA should remove all the unnecessary detritus of the distinction between short- and long-term capital gains, and between capital gains and other income, from the tax code and—more important—from the tax forms that people file.

Taxing capital gains and other income at the same low rates would produce significant gains in terms of economic efficiency. There would be no incentive to convert other income into realized capital gains.

Capital gains would no longer be an important element in tax shelter schemes.[3] With tax rates on ordinary income lower, there would also be less incentive to avoid tax by other means.

A broad base and low rates may not be enough by themselves, however. The existence of a multiplicity of financial instruments will tend to subvert the realization principle over time.[4] That is, people will be able to endlessly defer realizing taxable gains and will have a strong incentive to convert other income into capital gains, because the latter could never be taxed.

In addition, there is an argument for taxing capital gains on corporate stock at lower rates than other capital gains if full corporate integration is infeasible. To the extent that gains on stock reflect retained earnings, they have already been taxed at the corporate level. When realized capital gains were fully taxed, some economists suggested that tax rates be cut on capital gains on publicly traded corporate stock, held either directly or indirectly through mutual funds.[5]

Both concerns could be addressed if capital gains on corporate stock were taxed on an accrual basis and indexed for inflation. This option would partly offset the double tax on corporate stock, without creating a significant opening for tax shelters. Tax shelters require that tax losses and credits be passed through to the owner of the tax-shelter investment. This would not be possible if the asset were held in corporate form. The corporate income tax would also discourage using a corporate shell as a conduit for tax-shelter income. Finally, the fact that the stock has to be publicly traded would also deter abuse.

Taxing corporate stock on an accrual basis would end lock-in, because tax liability would be unaffected by when the asset is sold. That would be feasible for stock because the value is easily determined. As long as the gain is taxed as it accrues, taxpayers cannot realize gains and defer losses. Thus they could fully deduct any losses against other income, which would encourage risk-taking. Moreover, indexing capital gains on an accrual basis would be a nearly perfect correction for the effects of inflation, reducing risk still further.

Another advantage of real accrual taxation for corporate stock is that taxes would no longer discourage firms from paying out their earnings in the form of dividends. Assuming that dividend payments are reflected in the price of stock, total tax liability (on dividends plus capital gains) would be unaffected by dividend payouts, since a higher dividend would translate into smaller capital gain.[6] As long as real gains and dividends are taxed at the same rate, the total tax bill would not be affected by dividend distribution policy. Although this is still an imperfect solution as long as interest expense is unindexed, the income tax is unlikely to be perfected any time soon. Nevertheless, it would be nice to move it in the right direction.

SCHEDULE D
AND INSTRUCTIONS

The complexity of capital gains taxation is apparent from the tax form on which capital gains are reported, Schedule D, and the associated IRS instructions, which are reproduced in this appendix. The instructions provide more technical details about the definition of capital assets and the treatment of capital gains than are given in the text. Even more information and examples, as well as current versions of tax forms and instructions, are available free from the IRS in Publications 544 ("Sales and Other Dispositions of Assets") and 550 ("Investment Income and Expenses"). The IRS website address is http://www.irs.ustreas.gov/.

154 ■ SCHEDULE D AND INSTRUCTIONS

SCHEDULE D (Form 1040)

Department of the Treasury (U)
Internal Revenue Service

Capital Gains and Losses

▶ Attach to Form 1040. ▶ See Instructions for Schedule D (Form 1040).
▶ Use Schedule D-1 for more space to list transactions for lines 1 and 8.

OMB No. 1545-0074

1998

Attachment
Sequence No. **12**

Name(s) shown on Form 1040

Your social security number

Part I — Short-Term Capital Gains and Losses—Assets Held One Year or Less

(a) Description of property (Example: 100 sh. XYZ Co.)	(b) Date acquired (Mo., day, yr.)	(c) Date sold (Mo., day, yr.)	(d) Sales price (see page D-6)	(e) Cost or other basis (see page D-6)	(f) GAIN or (LOSS) Subtract (e) from (d)
1					

2 Enter your short-term totals, if any, from Schedule D-1, line 2 . . . . **2**

3 **Total short-term sales price amounts.** Add column (d) of lines 1 and 2 . . . **3**

4 Short-term gain from Form 6252 and short-term gain or (loss) from Forms 4684, 6781, and 8824 . . . . **4**

5 Net short-term gain or (loss) from partnerships, S corporations, estates, and trusts from Schedule(s) K-1 . . . . **5**

6 Short-term capital loss carryover. Enter the amount, if any, from line 8 of your 1997 Capital Loss Carryover Worksheet . . . . **6** (   )

7 **Net short-term capital gain or (loss).** Combine lines 1 through 6 in column (f). . . . . ▶ **7**

Part II — Long-Term Capital Gains and Losses—Assets Held More Than One Year

(a) Description of property (Example: 100 sh. XYZ Co.)	(b) Date acquired (Mo., day, yr.)	(c) Date sold (Mo., day, yr.)	(d) Sales price (see page D-6)	(e) Cost or other basis (see page D-6)	(f) GAIN or (LOSS) Subtract (e) from (d)	(g) 28% RATE GAIN or (LOSS) *(see instr. below)
8						

9 Enter your long-term totals, if any, from Schedule D-1, line 9 . . . . . . **9**

10 **Total long-term sales price amounts.** Add column (d) of lines 8 and 9 . . . **10**

11 Gain from Form 4797, Part I; long-term gain from Forms 2439 and 6252; and long-term gain or (loss) from Forms 4684, 6781, and 8824 . . . . . . **11**

12 Net long-term gain or (loss) from partnerships, S corporations, estates, and trusts from Schedule(s) K-1. . . . . . . **12**

13 Capital gain distributions. See page D-2 . . . . **13**

14 Long-term capital loss carryover. Enter in both columns (f) and (g) the amount, if any, from line 13 of your 1997 Capital Loss Carryover Worksheet . . . **14** (   ) (   )

15 Combine lines 8 through 14 in column (g) **15**

16 **Net long-term capital gain or (loss).** Combine lines 8 through 14 in column (f). . . . . ▶ **16**

Next: Go to Part III on the back.

*28% Rate Gain or Loss includes **all** "collectibles gains and losses" (as defined on page D-6) and up to 50% of the eligible gain on qualified small business stock (see page D-5).

For Paperwork Reduction Act Notice, see Form 1040 instructions.   Cat. No. 15787U   Schedule D (Form 1040) 1998

Schedule D (Form 1040) 1998   Page **2**

Part III   **Summary of Parts I and II**

17	Combine lines 7 and 16. If a loss, go to line 18. If a gain, enter the gain on Form 1040, line 13	**17**	
	Next: Complete Form 1040 through line 39. Then, go to **Part IV** to figure your tax if:		
	• Both lines 16 and 17 are gains, **and**		
	• Form 1040, line 39, is more than zero.		
18	If line 17 is a loss, enter here and as a (loss) on Form 1040, line 13, the **smaller** of these losses:		
	• The loss on line 17; **or**		
	• ($3,000) or, if married filing separately, ($1,500)	**18** (	)
	Next: Complete Form 1040 through line 37. Then, complete the **Capital Loss Carryover Worksheet** on page D-6 if:		
	• The loss on line 17 exceeds the loss on line 18, **or**		
	• Form 1040, line 37, is a loss.		

Part IV   **Tax Computation Using Maximum Capital Gains Rates**

19	Enter your taxable income from Form 1040, line 39		**19**	
20	Enter the **smaller** of line 16 or line 17 of Schedule D	**20**		
21	If you are filing Form 4952, enter the amount from Form 4952, line 4e	**21**		
22	Subtract line 21 from line 20	**22**		
23	Combine lines 7 and 15. If zero or less, enter -0-	**23**		
24	Enter the **smaller** of line 15 or line 23, but not less than zero . . .	**24**		
25	Enter your unrecaptured section 1250 gain, if any (see page D-7) .	**25**		
26	Add lines 24 and 25	**26**		
27	Subtract line 26 from line 22. If zero or less, enter -0-		**27**	
28	Subtract line 27 from line 19. If zero or less, enter -0-		**28**	
29	Enter the **smaller** of:			
	• The amount on line 19, **or**			
	• $25,350 if single; $42,350 if married filing jointly or qualifying widow(er); $21,175 if married filing separately; or $33,950 if head of household		**29**	
30	Enter the **smaller** of line 28 or line 29		**30**	
31	Subtract line 22 from line 19. If zero or less, enter -0-		**31**	
32	Enter the **larger** of line 30 or line 31		**32**	
33	Figure the tax on the amount on line 32. Use the Tax Table or Tax Rate Schedules, whichever applies . . . . ▶		**33**	
34	Enter the amount from line 29		**34**	
35	Enter the amount from line 28		**35**	
36	Subtract line 35 from line 34. If zero or less, enter -0-		**36**	
37	Multiply line 36 by 10% (.10) . . . . ▶		**37**	
38	Enter the **smaller** of line 19 or line 27		**38**	
39	Enter the amount from line 36		**39**	
40	Subtract line 39 from line 38		**40**	
41	Multiply line 40 by 20% (.20) . . . . ▶		**41**	
42	Enter the **smaller** of line 22 or line 25		**42**	
43	Add lines 22 and 32	**43**		
44	Enter the amount from line 19	**44**		
45	Subtract line 44 from line 43. If zero or less, enter -0-		**45**	
46	Subtract line 45 from line 42. If zero or less, enter -0-		**46**	
47	Multiply line 46 by 25% (.25) . . . . ▶		**47**	
48	Enter the amount from line 19		**48**	
49	Add lines 32, 36, 40, and 46		**49**	
50	Subtract line 49 from line 48		**50**	
51	Multiply line 50 by 28% (.28) . . . . ▶		**51**	
52	Add lines 33, 37, 41, 47, and 51		**52**	
53	Figure the tax on the amount on line 19. Use the Tax Table or Tax Rate Schedules, whichever applies		**53**	
54	**Tax on taxable income (including capital gains).** Enter the **smaller** of line 52 or line 53 here and on Form 1040, line 40 . . . . ▶		**54**	

✪ *Printed on recycled paper*   *U.S. Government Printing Office: 1998 — 435-557*

1998 Instructions for Schedule D, Capital Gains and Losses

Use Schedule D (Form 1040) to report:
- The sale or exchange of a capital asset (defined on this page).
- Gains from involuntary conversions (other than from casualty or theft) of capital assets not held for business or profit.
- Capital gain distributions.
- Nonbusiness bad debts.

Additional Information. See **Pub. 544** and **Pub. 550** for more details. For a comprehensive filled-in example of Schedule D, see Pub. 550.

Section references are to the Internal Revenue Code unless otherwise noted.

General Instructions

Changes To Note
- For sales, exchanges, and conversions after 1997, property held more than 1 year (instead of more than 18 months) generally is eligible for the 10%, 20%, and 25% maximum capital gains rates. This rule also applies to installment payments received after 1997. The 28% rate will now apply **only** to pre-1998 gains (e.g., from fiscal year partnerships and mutual funds), collectibles gains, and part or all of the gain from the sale or exchange of qualified small business stock.
- If you sold qualified small business stock held more than 5 years, you may be able to exclude up to 50% of the gain. See page D-5 for details.

Other Forms You May Have To File
Use **Form 4797** to report the following:
- The sale or exchange of property used in a trade or business; depreciable and amortizable property; oil, gas, geothermal, or other mineral property; and section 126 property.
- The involuntary conversion (other than from casualty or theft) of property used in a trade or business and capital assets held for business or profit.
- The disposition of noncapital assets other than inventory or property held primarily for sale to customers in the ordinary course of your trade or business.
- Ordinary loss on the sale, exchange, or worthlessness of small business investment company (section 1242) stock.
- Ordinary loss on the sale, exchange, or worthlessness of small business (section 1244) stock.

Use **Form 4684** to report involuntary conversions of property due to casualty or theft.

Use **Form 6781** to report gains and losses from section 1256 contracts and straddles.

Use **Form 8824** if you made one or more "like-kind" exchanges. A like-kind exchange occurs when you exchange business or investment property for property of a like kind. For exchanges of capital assets, include the gain or (loss) from Form 8824, if any, on line 4 or line 11.

Capital Asset
Most property you own and use for personal purposes, pleasure, or investment is a capital asset. For example, your house, furniture, car, stocks, and bonds are capital assets. A capital asset is any property held by you **except** the following:

1. Stock in trade or other property included in inventory or held for sale to customers.

2. Accounts or notes receivable for services performed in the ordinary course of your trade or business or as an employee, or from the sale of any property described in **1.**

3. Depreciable property used in your trade or business even if it is fully depreciated.

4. Real estate used in your trade or business.

5. Copyrights, literary, musical, or artistic compositions, letters or memoranda, or similar property: **(a)** created by your personal efforts; **(b)** prepared or produced for you (in the case of letters, memoranda, or similar property); or **(c)** that you received from someone who created them or for whom they were created, as mentioned in **(a)** or **(b)**, in a way (such as by gift) that entitled you to the basis of the previous owner.

6. U.S. Government publications, including the Congressional Record, that you received from the government, other than by purchase at the normal sales price, or that you got from someone who had received it in a similar way,

if your basis is determined by reference to the previous owner's basis.

Capital Assets Held for Personal Use
Gain from the sale or exchange of this property is a capital gain. Report it on Schedule D, Part I or Part II. Loss from the sale or exchange of this property is not deductible. But if you had a loss from the sale or exchange of real estate held for personal use for which you received a **Form 1099-S**, you must report the transaction on Schedule D even though the loss is not deductible.

For example, you have a loss on the sale of a vacation home that is not your main home. Report it on line 1 or 8, depending on how long you owned the home. Complete columns (a) through (e). Because the loss is not deductible, enter -0- in column (f).

Short Term or Long Term
Separate your capital gains and losses according to how long you held or owned the property. The holding period for short-term capital gains and losses is 1 year or less. The holding period for long-term capital gains and losses is more than 1 year. To figure the holding period, begin counting on the day after you received the property and include the day you disposed of it.

If you disposed of property that you acquired by inheritance, report the disposition as a long-term gain or loss, regardless of how long you held the property.

A nonbusiness bad debt must be treated as a short-term capital loss. See Pub. 550 for what qualifies as a nonbusiness bad debt and how to enter it on Schedule D.

Partnership Interests
A sale or other disposition of an interest in a partnership may result in ordinary income or unrecaptured section 1250 gain. See **Pub. 541** and the worksheet for line 25 on page D-7.

Capital Gain Distributions

Enter on line 13, column (f), the **total** capital gain distributions paid to you during the year, regardless of how long you held your investment. Enter on line 13, column (g), the total of the amounts reported to you as the 28% rate gain portion of your total capital gain distributions. See below for a filled-in example of how to report capital gain distributions.

If you have an amount in box 2c, see the worksheet for line 25 on page D-7. If you have an amount in box 2d, see **Exclusion of Gain on Qualified Small Business Stock (Section 1202)** on page D-5.

If you received capital gain distributions as a nominee (that is, they were paid to you but actually belong to someone else), report only the amount that belongs to you on line 13. Attach a statement showing

the full amount you received and the amount you received as a nominee. See page B-1 for filing requirements for Forms 1099-DIV and 1096.

Note: *The example below is for a taxpayer whose only capital gains are capital gain distributions from a mutual fund (or other regulated investment company). If you have other capital gains or losses, you will have to complete additional lines on page 1 of Schedule D.*

FIRST . . . Enter the total amounts from all your Forms 1099-DIV (or substitute statements), boxes 2a and 2b, on Schedule D, line 13, columns (f) and (g), respectively.

THEN . . . Complete lines 15 and 16, and go to Part III on the back of Schedule D.

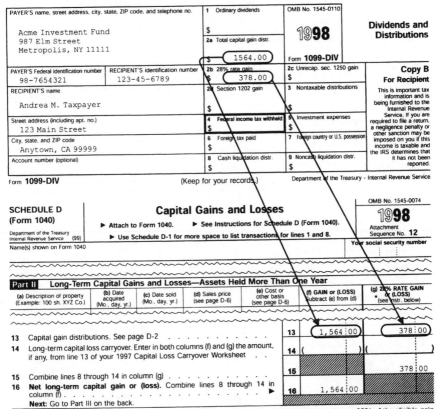

13	Capital gain distributions. See page D-2	**13**	1,564 00	378 00
14	Long-term capital loss carryover. Enter in both columns (f) and (g) the amount, if any, from line 13 of your 1997 Capital Loss Carryover Worksheet . .	**14**	( )	( )
15	Combine lines 8 through 14 in column (g)	**15**		378 00
16	**Net long-term capital gain or (loss).** Combine lines 8 through 14 in column (f) . . . . ▶	**16**	1,564 00	

Next: Go to Part III on the back.

* **28% Rate Gain or Loss** includes **all** "collectibles gains and losses" (as defined on page D-7) and up to 50% of the eligible gain on qualified small business stock (see page D-5).

For Paperwork Reduction Act Notice, see Form 1040 instructions.   Cat. No. 11338H   Schedule D (Form 1040) 1998

D-2

Sale of Your Home

If you sold or exchanged your main home in 1998, do not report it on your tax return unless your gain exceeds your exclusion amount. Generally, if you meet the two tests below, you can exclude up to $250,000 of gain. If both you and your spouse meet these tests, and you file a joint return, you can exclude up to $500,000 of gain (but only one spouse needs to meet the ownership requirement in **Test 1**).

Test 1. You owned and used the home as your main home for 2 years or more during the 5-year period ending on the date you sold or exchanged your home.

Test 2. You have not sold or exchanged another main home during the 2-year period ending on the date of sale or exchange of your home (not counting any sales or exchanges before May 7, 1997).

See **Pub. 523** for details, including how to report any taxable gain on Schedule D, if:

• You do not meet one of the above two tests,

• You (or your spouse if married) used any part of the home for business or rental purposes after May 6, 1997, **or**

• Your gain exceeds your exclusion amount.

Note: *Form 2119, which was previously used to report home sales, is now obsolete.*

Nondeductible Losses

Do not deduct a loss from the direct or indirect sale or exchange of property between any of the following.

• Members of a family.

• A corporation and an individual owning more than 50% of the corporation's stock (unless the loss is from a distribution in complete liquidation of a corporation).

• A grantor and a fiduciary of a trust.

• A fiduciary and a beneficiary of the same trust.

• A fiduciary and a beneficiary of another trust created by the same grantor.

• An executor of an estate and a beneficiary of that estate, unless the sale or exchange was to satisfy a pecuniary bequest (i.e., a bequest of a sum of money).

• An individual and a tax-exempt organization controlled by the individual or the individual's family.

See Pub. 544 for more details on sales and exchanges between related parties.

If you disposed of **(a)** an asset used in an activity to which the at-risk rules apply or **(b)** any part of your interest in an activity to which the at-risk rules apply, and you have amounts in the activity for which you are not at risk, see the instructions for **Form 6198.**

If the loss is allowable under the at-risk rules, it may then be subject to the passive activity rules. See **Form 8582** and its instructions to see how to report capital gains and losses from a passive activity.

Items for Special Treatment

• Transactions by a securities dealer. See section 1236.

• Bonds and other debt instruments. See Pub. 550 for details.

• Certain real estate subdivided for sale that may be considered a capital asset. See section 1237.

• Gain on the sale of depreciable property to a more than 50% owned entity, or to a trust of which you are a beneficiary. See Pub. 544 for details.

• Gain on the disposition of stock in an interest charge domestic international sales corporation. See section 955(c).

• Gain on the sale or exchange of stock in certain foreign corporations. See section 1248.

• Transfer of property to a partnership that would be treated as an investment company if it were incorporated. See **Pub. 541.**

• Sales of stock received under a qualified public utility dividend reinvestment plan. See Pub. 550 for details.

• Transfer of appreciated property to a political organization. See section 84.

• In general, no gain or loss is recognized on the transfer of property from an individual to a spouse or a former spouse if the transfer is incident to a divorce. See **Pub. 504.**

• Amounts received on the retirement of a debt instrument generally are treated as received in exchange for the debt instrument. See Pub. 550.

• Any loss on the disposition of converted wetland or highly erodible cropland that is first used for farming after March 1, 1986, is reported as a long-term capital loss on Schedule D, but any gain is reported as ordinary income on Form 4797.

• Amounts received by shareholders in corporate liquidations. See Pub. 550.

• Cash received in lieu of fractional shares of stock as a result of a stock split or stock dividend. See Pub. 550 for details.

• Mutual fund load charges may not be taken into account in determining gain or loss on certain dispositions of stock in mutual funds if reinvestment rights were exercised. For details, see **Pub. 564.**

Wash Sales

A wash sale occurs when you sell or otherwise dispose of stock or securities (including a contract or option to acquire or sell stock or securities) at a loss and, within 30 days before or after the sale or disposition, you directly or indirectly:

• Buy substantially identical stock or securities,

• Acquire substantially identical stock or securities in a fully taxable trade, or

• Enter into a contract or option to acquire substantially identical stock or securities.

You **cannot** deduct losses from wash sales unless the loss was incurred in the ordinary course of your business as a dealer in stock or securities. The basis of the substantially identical property (or contract or option to acquire such property) is its cost increased by the disallowed loss. For more details on wash sales, see section 1091.

Report a wash sale transaction on line 1 or 8. Show the full amount of the (loss) in column (f). Directly below the line on which you reported the loss, enter "Wash Sale" in column (a) and the amount of the loss not allowed as a positive amount in column (f).

Short Sales

A short sale is a contract to sell property you borrowed for delivery to a buyer. At a later date, you either buy substantially identical property and deliver it to the lender or deliver the property that you held but did not want to transfer at the time of the sale. Usually, your holding period is the amount of time you actually held the property eventually delivered to the lender to close the short sale. However, your gain when closing a short sale is short term if you **(a)** held substantially identical property for 1 year or less on the date of the short sale, or **(b)** acquired property substantially identical to the property sold short after the short sale but on or before the date you close the short sale.

If you held substantially identical property for more than 1 year on the date of a short sale, any loss realized on the short sale is a long-term capital loss, even if the property used to close the short sale was held 1 year or less.

Constructive Sales Treatment for Certain Appreciated Positions

Generally, you must recognize gain (but not loss) on the date you enter into a constructive sale of any appreciated position in stock, a partnership interest, or certain debt instruments as if the position were disposed of at fair market value on that date.

You are treated as making a constructive sale of an appreciated position when you (or a related person, in some cases) do one of the following:

● Enter into a short sale of the same or substantially identical property (i.e., a "short sale against the box").

● Enter into an offsetting notional principal contract relating to the same or substantially identical property.

● Enter into a futures or forward contract to deliver the same or substantially identical property.

● Acquire the same or substantially identical property (if the appreciated position is a short sale, offsetting notional principal contract, or a futures or forward contract).

Exception. Generally, constructive sale treatment **does not** apply if:

● You closed the transaction before the end of the 30th day after the end of the year in which it was entered into,

● You held the appreciated position to which the transaction relates throughout the 60-day period starting on the date the transaction was closed, **and**

● At no time during that 60-day period was your risk of loss reduced by holding certain other positions.

For details and other exceptions to these rules, see Pub. 550.

Gain or Loss From Options

Report on Schedule D gain or loss from the closing or expiration of an option that is not a section 1256 contract, but that is a capital asset in your hands. If a purchased option expired, enter the expiration date in column (c) and enter **"EXPIRED"** in column (d). If an option that was granted (written) expired, enter the expiration date in column (b) and enter **"EXPIRED"** in column (e). Fill in the other columns as appropriate. See Pub. 550 for more details.

Sales of Stock to ESOPs or Certain Cooperatives

If you sold qualified securities (defined in section 1042(c)(1)) held for at least 3 years to an employee stock ownership plan (ESOP) or eligible worker-owned cooperative, you may be able to elect to postpone all or part of the gain on the sale if you bought qualified replacement property (securities) within the period that began 3 months before the sale and ended 12 months after the sale. If you make the election, you must recognize gain on the sale only to the extent the proceeds from the sale exceed the cost of the qualified replacement property. You must reduce the basis of the replacement property by any postponed gain. If you dispose of any replacement property, you may have to recognize all of the postponed gain.

Generally, to qualify for the election, the ESOP or cooperative must own immediately after the sale at least 30% of the outstanding stock of the corporation that issued the qualified securities. Also, the qualified replacement property must have been issued by a domestic operating corporation.

Similar rules apply to the sale of stock of a qualified refiner or processor to an eligible farmers' cooperative. See section 1042(g) for details and exceptions.

You must make the election no later than the due date (including extensions) for filing your tax return for the year in which you sold the stock. To make the election, report the entire gain realized on the sale on line 8. Directly below the line on which you reported the gain, enter in column (a) "Section 1042 election" and enter as a (loss) in column (f) the amount of the gain you are postponing or expect to postpone. If the actual postponed gain is different from what you expected, file an amended return.

Also attach the following statements:

1. A "statement of election" that indicates you are making an election under section 1042(a) and that includes the following information: **(a)** a description of the securities sold, the date of sale, the amount realized on the sale, and the adjusted basis of the qualified securities; **(b)** the name of the ESOP or cooperative to which the qualified securities were sold; and **(c)** for a sale that was part of a single, interrelated transaction under a prearranged agreement between taxpayers involving other sales of qualified securities, the names and identifying numbers of the other taxpayers under the agreement and the number of shares sold by the other taxpayers.

2. A notarized "statement of purchase" describing the qualified replacement property, date of purchase, and the cost of the property, and declaring the property to be qualified replacement property for the qualified stock you sold. The statement must have been notarized no later than 30 days after the purchase. If you have not yet purchased the qualified replacement property, you must attach the notarized "statement of purchase" to your income tax return for the year following the election year (or the election will not be valid).

3. A verified written statement of the domestic corporation whose employees are covered by the ESOP acquiring the qualified securities, or of any authorized officer of the cooperative, consenting to the taxes under sections 4978 and 4979A on certain dispositions and prohibited allocations of the stock purchased by the ESOP or cooperative.

For details, see section 1042 and Temporary Regulations section 1.1042-1T.

Specialized Small Business Investment Companies (SSBICs)

If you sold publicly traded securities, you may be able to postpone all or part of the gain on that sale if you bought common stock or a partnership interest in an SSBIC during the 60-day period that began on the date of the sale. An SSBIC is any partnership or corporation licensed by the Small Business Administration under section 301(d) of the Small Business Investment Act of 1958. You must recognize gain to the extent the sale proceeds exceed the cost of your SSBIC stock or partnership interest purchased during the 60-day period that began on the date of the sale and not previously taken into account). The gain you postpone is limited to $50,000 a year and $500,000 during your lifetime (reduce these amounts by one-half if you are married filing separately). Reduce the basis of your SSBIC stock or partnership interest by any postponed gain. If you choose to postpone gain, report the entire gain realized on the sale on line 1 or 8. Directly below the line on which you reported the gain, enter in column (a) "SSBIC Rollover" and enter as a (loss) in column (f) the amount of the postponed gain. Also attach a schedule showing **(a)** how you figured the postponed gain, **(b)** the name of the SSBIC in which you purchased common stock or a partnership interest, **(c)** the date of that purchase, and **(d)** your new basis in that SSBIC stock or partnership interest.

Exclusion of Gain on Qualified Small Business Stock (Section 1202)

Section 1202 allows for an exclusion of up to 50% of the eligible gain on the sale or exchange of qualified small business stock. The section 1202 exclusion applies only to qualified small business stock issued after August 10, 1993, and held for more than 5 years. To be **qualified small business stock,** the stock must meet **all** of the following tests:

● It must be stock in a C corporation (i.e., not S corporation stock).

● It must have been originally issued after August 10, 1993.

● As of the date the stock was issued, the corporation was a qualified small business. A qualified small business is a domestic C corporation with total gross assets of $50 million or less **(a)** at all times after August 9, 1993, and before the stock was issued, and **(b)** immediately after the stock was issued. Gross assets include those of any predecessor of the corporation. All corporations that are members of the same parent-subsidiary controlled group are treated as one corporation.

● You must have acquired the stock at its original issue (either directly or through an underwriter), either in exchange for money or other property or as pay for services (other than as an underwriter) to the corporation. In certain cases, you may meet the test if you acquired the stock from another person who met the test (such as by gift or inheritance) or through a conversion or exchange of qualified small business stock you held.

● During substantially all the time you held the stock:

1. The corporation was a C corporation,

2. At least 80% of the value of the corporation's assets were used in the active conduct of one or more qualified businesses (defined below), and

3. The corporation **was not** a foreign corporation, DISC, former DISC, corporation that has made (or that has a subsidiary that has made) a section 936 election, regulated investment company, real estate investment trust, REMIC, FASIT, or cooperative.

Note: *A specialized small business investment company (SSBIC) is treated as having met tests 2 and 3 above.*

A **qualified business** is any business **other than** the following:

● One involving services performed in the fields of health, law, engineering, architecture, accounting, actuarial science, performing arts, consulting, athletics, financial services, or brokerage services.

● One whose principal asset is the reputation or skill of one or more employees.

● Any banking, insurance, financing, leasing, investing, or similar business.

● Any farming business (including the raising or harvesting of trees).

● Any business involving the production of products for which percentage depletion can be claimed.

● Any business of operating a hotel, motel, restaurant, or similar business.

For more details about limits and additional requirements that may apply, see section 1202.

Pass-Through Entities

If you held an interest in a pass-through entity (a partnership, S corporation, or mutual fund or other regulated investment company) that sold qualified small business stock, you must have held the interest on the date the pass-through entity acquired the qualified small business stock and at all times thereafter until the stock was sold to qualify for the exclusion.

How To Report

Report in column (f) of line 8 the entire gain realized on the sale of qualified small business stock. In column (g) of line 8, report as 28% rate gain an amount equal to the section 1202 exclusion. Directly below the line on which you reported the gain, enter in column (a) "Section 1202 exclusion" and enter as a (loss) in column (f) the amount of the allowable exclusion.

Gain From Form 1099-DIV. If you received a Form 1099-DIV with a gain in box 2d, part or all of that gain (which is also included in box 2a) may be eligible for the section 1202 exclusion. In column (a) of line 8, enter the name of the corporation whose stock was sold. In column (f), enter the amount of your allowable exclusion as a loss. In column (g), enter the amount of your allowable exclusion as a gain.

Gain From Form 2439. If you received a Form 2439 with a gain in box 1d, part or all of that gain (which is also included in box 1a) may be eligible for the section 1202 exclusion. In column (a) of line 8, enter the name of the corporation whose stock was sold. In column (f), enter the amount of your allowable exclusion as a loss. In column (g), enter the amount of your allowable exclusion as a gain.

Alternative Minimum Tax. You must include 42% of the exclusion amount on **Form 6251,** line 14m. Complete Form 6251 to see if you owe this tax.

Rollover of Gain From Qualified Stock

If you sold qualified small business stock (defined above) that you held for more than 6 months, you may postpone gain if you purchase other qualified small business stock during the 60-day period that began on the date of the sale. You must recognize gain to the extent the sale proceeds exceed the cost of the replacement stock. Reduce the basis of the replacement stock by any postponed gain. If you choose to postpone gain, report the entire gain realized on the sale on line 1 or 8. Directly below the line on which you reported the gain, enter in column (a) "Section 1045 Rollover" and enter as a (loss) in column (f) the amount of the postponed gain.

Undistributed Capital Gains

Include on line 11, column (f), the amount from box 1a of **Form 2439.** This represents your share of the undistributed long-term capital gains of the regulated investment company (mutual fund) or real estate investment trust.

Include on line 11, column (g), the amount, if any, from box 1b of Form 2439. If there is an amount in box 1c of Form 2439, see the worksheet for line 25 on page D-7. If there is an amount in box 1d of Form 2439, see **Exclusion of Gain on Qualified Small Business Stock (Section 1202)** on this page.

Enter on Form 1040, line 63, the tax paid as shown in box 2 of Form 2439. Add to the basis of your stock the excess of the amount included in income over the amount of the credit for the tax paid. See Pub. 550 for more details.

Installment Sales

If you sold property (other than publicly traded stocks or securities) at a gain and you will receive a payment in a tax year after the year of sale, you must report the sale on the installment method unless you elect not to. Use **Form 6252** to report the sale on the installment method. Also use Form 6252 to report any payment received in 1998 from a sale made in an earlier year that you reported on the installment method. To elect out of the installment method, report the full amount of the gain on Schedule D on a timely filed return (including extensions).

Specific Instructions

Column (b)—Date Acquired

Enter in this column the date the asset was acquired. Use the trade date for stocks and bonds traded on an exchange or over-the-counter market. For stock or other property sold short, enter the date the stock or property was delivered to the broker or lender to close the short sale.

If you disposed of property that you acquired by inheritance, report the gain or (loss) on line 8 and enter **"INHERIT-ED"** in column (b) instead of the date you acquired the property.

If you sold a block of stock (or similar property) that was acquired through several different purchases, you may report the sale on one line and enter **"VARIOUS"** in column (b). However, you still must report the short-term gain or (loss) in Part I and the long-term gain or (loss) in Part II.

Column (c)—Date Sold

Enter in this column the date the asset was sold. Use the trade date for stocks and bonds traded on an exchange or over-the-counter market. For stock or other property sold short, enter the date you sold the stock or property you borrowed to open the short sale transaction.

Column (d)—Sales Price

Enter in this column either the gross sales price or the net sales price from the sale. If you sold stocks or bonds and you received a Form 1099-B or similar statement from your broker that shows gross sales price, enter that amount in column (d). But if Form 1099-B (or your broker) indicates that gross proceeds minus commissions and option premiums were reported to the IRS, enter that net amount in column (d). If the net amount is entered in column (d), **do not** include the commissions and option premiums from the sale in column (e).

You should not have received a Form 1099-B (or substitute statement) for a transaction merely representing the return of your original investment in a nontransferable obligation, such as a savings bond or a certificate of deposit. But if you did, report the amount shown on Form 1099-B (or substitute statement) in both columns (d) and (e).

Caution: Be sure to add all sales price entries on lines 1 and 8, column (d), to amounts on lines 2 and 9, column (d). Enter the totals on lines 3 and 10.

Column (e)—Cost or Other Basis

In general, the cost or other basis is the cost of the property plus purchase commissions and improvements, minus depreciation, amortization, and depletion. If you inherited the property, got it as a gift, or received it in a tax-free exchange, involuntary conversion, or "wash sale" of stock, you may not be able to use the actual cost as the basis. If you do not use the actual cost, attach an explanation of your basis.

When selling stock, adjust your basis by subtracting all the nontaxable distributions you received before the sale. Also adjust your basis for any stock splits. See Pub. 550 for details on how to figure your basis in stock that split while you owned it.

You can choose to use an average basis for mutual fund shares if you acquired the shares at various times and prices and you left the shares on deposit in an account handled by a custodian or agent who acquired or redeemed those shares. For details on how to figure average basis, see **Pub. 564.**

The basis of property acquired by gift is generally the basis of the property in the hands of the donor. The basis of property acquired from a decedent is generally the fair market value at the date of death. See Pub. 544 for details.

Increase the cost or other basis of an original issue discount (OID) debt instrument by the amount of OID that has been included in gross income for that instrument.

If a charitable contribution deduction is allowed because of a bargain sale of property to a charitable organization, the adjusted basis for purposes of determining gain from the sale is the amount which has the same ratio to the adjusted basis as the amount realized has to the fair market value.

Increase your cost or other basis by any expense of sale, such as broker's fees, commissions, state and local transfer taxes, and option premiums, before making an entry in column (e), unless you reported the net sales price in column (d).

For more details, see **Pub. 551.**

Capital Loss Carryover Worksheet—Line 18
(keep for your records)

Use this worksheet to figure your capital loss carryovers from 1998 to 1999 if Schedule D, line 18, is a loss and **(a)** that loss is a smaller loss than the loss on Schedule D, line 17, **or (b)** Form 1040, line 37, is a loss. Otherwise, you do not have any carryovers.

1. Enter the amount from Form 1040, line 37. If a loss, enclose the amount in parentheses . . . .   **1.** _____

2. Enter the loss from Schedule D, line 18, as a positive amount . . . .   **2.** _____

3. Combine lines 1 and 2. If zero or less, enter -0- . . .   **3.** _____

4. Enter the **smaller** of line 2 or line 3 . . . .   **4.** _____

    Note: If line 7 of Schedule D is a loss, go to line 5; otherwise, enter -0- on line 5 and go to line 9.

5. Enter the loss from Schedule D, line 7, as a positive amount . . . .   **5.** _____

6. Enter any gain from Schedule D, line 16   **6.** _____

7. Add lines 4 and 6 . . . .   **7.** _____

8. **Short-term capital loss carryover to 1999.** Subtract line 7 from line 5. If zero or less, enter -0-. . . . . . .   **8.** _____

    Note: If line 16 of Schedule D is a loss, go to line 9; otherwise, skip lines 9 through 13.

9. Enter the loss from Schedule D, line 16, as a positive amount . . . .   **9.** _____

10. Enter any gain from Schedule D, line 7   **10.** _____

11. Subtract line 5 from line 4. If zero or less, enter -0- . . . .   **11.** _____

12. Add lines 10 and 11 . . . .   **12.** _____

13. **Long-term capital loss carryover to 1999.** Subtract line 12 from line 9. If zero or less, enter -0- . . . . . .   **13.** _____

D-6

Column (f)—Gain or (Loss)

You **must** make a separate entry in this column for each transaction reported on lines 1 and 8 and any other line(s) that applies to you. For lines 1 and 8, subtract the amount in column (e) from the amount in column (d). Enter negative amounts in parentheses.

Column (g)—28% Rate Gain or (Loss)

Enter in column (g) **only** the amount, if any, from Part II, column (f) that is equal to the amount of your section 1202 exclusion from the eligible gain on qualified small business stock (see page D-5) or from collectibles gains and losses. A **collectibles gain or loss** is any long-term gain or loss from the sale or exchange of a collectible that is a capital asset.

Collectibles include works of art, rugs, antiques, metals (such as gold, silver, and platinum bullion), gems, stamps, coins, alcoholic beverages, and certain other tangible property.

Also include gain from the sale of an interest in a partnership, S corporation, or trust attributable to unrealized appreciation of collectibles.

Lines 1 and 8

Enter all sales and exchanges of capital assets, including stocks, bonds, etc., and real estate (if not reported on Form 4684, 4797, 6252, 6781, or 8824). Include these transactions even if you did not receive a **Form 1099-B** or **1099-S** (or substitute statement) for the transaction. You can use abbreviations to describe the property as long as they are based on the descriptions of the property as shown on Form 1099-B or 1099-S (or substitute statement).

Use **Schedule D-1** if you need more space to list transactions for lines 1 and 8. Use as many Schedules D-1 as you need. Enter on Schedule D, lines 2 and 9, the combined totals from all your Schedules D-1.

Caution: *Add the following amounts reported to you for 1998 on Forms 1099-B and 1099-S (or substitute statements):* **(a)** *proceeds from transactions involving stocks, bonds, and other securities, and* **(b)** *gross proceeds from real estate transactions not reported on another form or schedule. If this total is* **more** *than the total of lines 3 and 10, attach an explanation of the difference.*

Unrecaptured Section 1250 Gain Worksheet—Line 25
(keep for your records)

Note: *For each section 1250 property in Part III of Form 4797 for which you had an entry in column (g), but not in column (h), of Part I of Form 4797, complete lines 1 through 3. If you had more than one such property, complete lines 1 through 3 for each property on a separate worksheet. Enter the total of the line 3 amounts for all properties on line 3 and go to line 4. If your only unrecaptured section 1250 gain was from a partnership or an S corporation, go to line 4. If your only unrecaptured section 1250 gain was from an estate, trust, real estate investment trust, or mutual fund (or other regulated investment company), go to line 11.*

1. If you had a section 1250 property in Part III of Form 4797 for which you had an entry in column (g), but not in column (h), of Part I of Form 4797, enter the **smaller** of line 22 or line 24 of Form 4797 for that property . . **1.** _____

2. Enter the amount from Form 4797, line 26g, for the property for which you made an entry on line 1 . . . **2.** _____

3. Subtract line 2 from line 1 . . . . **3.** _____

4. Enter the total of any amounts reported to you on Schedules K-1 from a partnership or an S corporation as "unrecaptured section 1250 gain." Also include gain from the sale of an interest in a partnership attributable to unrecaptured section 1250 gain . . . . . . **4.** _____

5. Add lines 3 and 4 . . . . **5.** _____

6. Enter the smaller of line 5 or the gain, if any, from Form 4797, line 7, column (g) . . . . **6.** _____

   Note: *If you did not have an entry on Form 4797, line 8, enter the amount from line 6 above on line 10 below and go to line 11 below.*

7. Enter the amount from Form 4797, line 8, column (g) . . . . **7.** _____

8. Enter the amount from Form 4797, line 8, column (h) . . . . **8.** _____

9. Subtract line 8 from line 7 . . . . **9.** _____

10. Subtract line 9 from line 6 . . . . **10.** _____

11. Enter the total of any amounts reported to you on Schedules K-1 and Forms 1099-DIV and 2439 as "unrecaptured section 1250 gain" from an estate, trust, real estate investment trust, or mutual fund (or other regulated investment company) . . . . **11.** _____

12. Add lines 10 and 11 . . . . **12.** _____

13. Enter the gain or (loss) from Schedule D, line 15 . . . . **13.** _____

14. Enter the (loss), if any, from Schedule D, line 7. If Schedule D, line 7, is zero or a gain, enter -0- . . . . **14.** _____

15. Combine lines 13 and 14.
    ● If the result is zero or a gain, enter -0-.
    ● If the result is a (loss), enter it as a positive amount . **15.** _____

16. Subtract line 15 from line 12. If zero or less, enter -0-. Enter the result on Schedule D, line 25 . . . . . . **16.** _____

B

HOW SAVING AND INVESTMENT RESPOND TO HIGHER RATES OF RETURN

uppose that equilibrium saving and investment are determined by the simple interaction of the demand for saving (that is, investment demand) and the supply of saving. Four pieces of information are required to calculate the change in saving and investment in equilibrium: (1) the wedge between the cost of capital for businesses and the after-tax rate of return to investors, (2) how responsive investment is to the cost of capital, (3) how responsive private saving is to the rate of return, and (4) the effect of a tax cut on the deficit.

The responsiveness of national saving and investment to changes in the rate of return may be expressed numerically as elasticities: that is, the percentage change in saving or investment resulting from a 1 percent change in the rate of return or cost of capital, respectively. The interaction of the factors affecting equilibrium saving and investment may then be expressed as follows:

$$(\text{B-1}) \qquad \Delta S = \frac{\epsilon_d}{\epsilon_d - \epsilon_s} \left[\epsilon_s \times \frac{\Delta r}{r} \times S + \Delta D \right],$$

where ΔS is the change in equilibrium saving, ϵ_d is the elasticity of demand for investment, ϵ_s is the elasticity of supply of savings, $\Delta r/r$ is the proportional reduction in the cost of capital effected by the tax cut, S is the initial level of savings, and ΔD is the change in the deficit due to the reduction in taxes. Empirical evidence, discussed in chapter 4, is consistent with a demand elasticity of about -1.0, and a supply elasticity of 0 to 0.4. The first term in the brackets is the movement along the supply curve caused by the higher return to saving. The second term is the effect of a larger deficit or smaller surplus on public saving. Thus the equation says that a capital gains tax cut will increase or reduce equilibrium saving and investment depending on whether the response of private saving is greater or less than the response of public saving. The factor multiplying the expression in brackets reflects the effect of movement along the investment demand curve to the new equilibrium. If investment is highly responsive (ϵ_d is large in absolute value), the saving effect translates directly into greater investment. If investment demand is unresponsive, changes in private saving or the deficit have little effect on investment. Assuming a demand elasticity of -1.0 and a supply elasticity of 0.4, the equation would suggest that the change in equilibrium investment would be about three-quarters of the change in desired net saving (private and public).

Equation B-1 may be used to estimate approximately the effect of an illustrative cut in the tax rate on capital gains on national saving and investment, given assumptions about the key parameters. According to Congressional Budget Office (CBO) forecasts, personal saving will amount to $1,654 billion in the period 1997–2001. The Joint Committee on Taxation estimates that a 50 percent exclusion would have reduced federal revenues by $14.3 billion during the same period. Over the ten years from 1977 to 2006, saving is expected to total $3,901 billion, and the revenue cost $63.6 billion. The net change in savings and investment is calculated using equation B-1 for four different assumptions about how saving responds to higher rates of return (see table 4-1).

THE FUNDAMENTAL IDENTIFYING ASSUMPTION BEHIND CROSS-SECTIONAL ECONOMETRIC STUDIES IS INVALID

How much do individuals' tax rates vary from year to year? In order for cross-sectional econometric studies to measure a response to policy, rather than timing, individuals' tax rates must be roughly constant over time. In fact, they are highly volatile.[1]

Marginal tax rates for individual taxpayers traced over the five years from 1979 to 1983 vary substantially, and the variance increases over time, even after controlling for the effect of the major tax legislation in 1981, as illustrated in figure C-1. To create figure C-1, taxpayers were divided into ten groups that correspond to deciles of the unconditional sample distribution of first-dollar capital gains tax rates in 1979.[2] The figure is based on first-dollar tax rates because they are independent of individuals' decisions about how much capital gains to realize. Many econometric studies of capital gains use first-dollar tax rates as instruments for actual tax rates.

Each decile group was followed through 1983 to examine how closely the group's conditional distribution in following years corresponded to the unconditional distribution of first-dollar capital gains tax rates for each year. In figure C-1, the distribution of each group is represented by its quartiles. A tendency for the conditional quartiles to approach the unconditional quartiles quickly would indicate a high degree of intertemporal variation in first-dollar tax rates for each taxpayer. If the

Figure C-1. Intertemporal Variation of First-Dollar Marginal Tax Rates on Gains (Quartiles in 1979 to 1983 Conditional on Decile in 1979)[a]

Percentile of unconditional marginal tax rate distribution

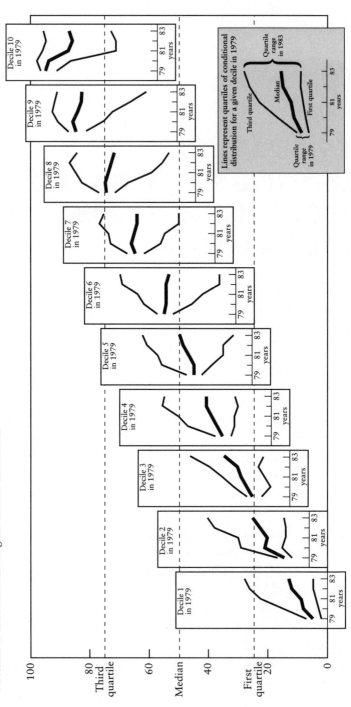

Source: Leonard E. Burman and William C. Randolph, "Measuring Permanent Responses to Capital Gains Taxes in Panel Data," Department of the Treasury, OTA Paper 68 (August 1994).

a. The graph is based on a weighted sample of taxpayers who realized gains in at least one year between 1979 and 1983. Taxpayers were sorted according to their first-dollar marginal tax rate in 1979. The lines show how the distribution of marginal tax rates changed over the five years of the panel.

conditional distributions remained relatively fixed, however, this would suggest that most variation in tax rates represents permanent differences among taxpayers.

For each of the ten decile groups, figure C-1 displays three lines that show how the first, second (median), and third quartiles of their conditional distributions are related to the percentiles of the unconditional distribution in each of the five years from 1979 through 1983. For example, consider taxpayers in the first decile of the unconditional distribution in 1979, represented by the left-most panel of the figure. By construction, the median for the first decile in 1979 corresponds to percentile 5 of the unconditional distribution; the first and third quartiles of the conditional distribution correspond to percentiles 2 and 7 of the unconditional distribution. After five years, however, the first, second, and third quartiles of the conditional distribution for the first group equaled percentiles 5, 13, and 28 of the unconditional distribution. Similarly, figure C-1 shows that the three conditional quartiles for taxpayers who were in the fifth decile in 1979 equaled percentiles 42, 45, and 47 of the unconditional distribution, but changed to equal percentiles 30, 50, and 63 of the unconditional distribution by 1983.[3]

The graph shows that there was substantial intertemporal variation in first-dollar capital gains tax rates between 1979 and 1983. In all ten decile groups, the conditional distributions increased in dispersion noticeably over the five-year period. Furthermore, the tendency of conditional medians to drift toward the unconditional medians shows that taxpayers with low tax rates in 1979 were likely to have had unusually low tax rates, and that taxpayers with high rates in 1979 were likely to have been experiencing unusually high rates in that year.

While providing strong evidence of transitory volatility in tax rates, figure C-1 also illustrates that there are systematic differences in the permanent tax rates of different taxpayers. The distribution of the bottom five deciles remains below the population distribution for all five years, and the top five deciles remain above the population distribution. Were tax rates purely random (transitory), the conditional distributions would have equaled the population distribution in 1980 through 1983.

CAPITALIZATION EFFECTS OF LOWER TAX RATES ON CAPITAL GAINS

The maximum increase in asset value may be derived simply by assuming that the supply of assets that generate capital gains is fixed in the short run and that the after-tax rates of return on alternative assets are also fixed. In this simple static model, the value of a capital asset increases according to the following formula:

$$(D\text{-}1) \qquad \frac{A_1}{A_0} = \frac{(1-\alpha)(1-\tau_g') + \alpha(1-\tau_d)}{(1-\alpha)(1-\tau_g) + \alpha(1-\tau_d)},$$

where A_0 and A_1 are asset values before and after the tax change, respectively, α is the share of asset return that is paid in the form of dividends, τ_g is the original and τ_g' is the new tax rate on capital gains, and τ_d is the tax rate on dividends. Assume that α is one-third and does not change as a result of the tax change, and that τ_d corresponds to a federal tax rate of 39.6 percent plus a state tax rate of 6 percent, less the federal tax deductibility (yielding a total effective rate of 43.6 percent). The statutory federal plus state marginal tax rate on capital gains for the highest-income individuals is 31.6 percent (assuming a 6 percent state tax rate). Under a 50 percent federal exclusion, it would be 23.4 percent (assuming that the state tax rate does not change). Accounting for the deferral of capital gains and the non-taxation of gains at death, the effective tax rates would have been about τ_g = 15.8 percent before passage of TRA97, and τ_g' = 11.7 percent with a 50 percent exclusion. Assuming further that the price of capital assets is determined by high-income individual investors who realize capital gains on their assets every year, asset values might increase by as much as 3.6 percent as a result of a 50 percent exclusion.

There are several reasons why the actual increase in price would be much smaller than this estimate. The price of capital assets is not determined by the average effective capital gains tax rate of individual investors, but as an equilibrium process in which taxable and nontaxable investors (such as pension funds and foreigners) adjust their portfolios so that their marginal risk-adjusted after-tax rates of return are the same for each asset in their portfolios. As asset prices increase, the quantity of those assets demanded by investors who are not subject to the income tax—or who are taxed at lower rates than the maximum—declines. At the same time, taxable individuals who purchase more capital gains–producing assets will require higher rates of return to compensate for the additional risk. The result is that pretax rates of return cannot fall by as much as predicted by the static model, and asset values cannot increase by as much. Indeed, if the supply of capital by untaxed investors is highly elastic and they are still holding assets that produce capital gains after the tax change, the change in asset prices—even in the short run—could be negligible.

Even if taxable individuals were the only participants in the market, the price would increase by less than the amount predicted by equation D-1. The equilibrium rate of return for assets that do not produce capital gains such as bonds would have to increase, which would reduce the increase in prices for capital gains assets. If saving is unresponsive, as suggested by the empirical literature, the effect of a capital gains tax cut would be primarily to reallocate capital from non-gains assets (bonds) to gains assets (stocks). If the demand for bond financing was highly elastic, then, in equilibrium, a large amount of capital could switch from bonds to stocks with little overall effect on the price of stocks. This conversion of ordinary income into gains corresponds to an indirect revenue cost from the tax change. Yet another factor tempering the price increase on stocks is the fact that investment in stocks is riskier than investment in bonds. Therefore, after-tax returns on stocks would have to increase to attract the additional capital away from bonds.

MEASURING AND MISMEASURING THE WELFARE GAIN TO INDIVIDUALS OF CAPITAL GAINS TAX CUTS

A reduction in capital gains tax rates generates a consumer surplus for investors in much the same way that a decline in price produces a surplus for consumers. The relationship between realizations of capital gains and the tax rate may be expressed as a sort of consumer demand curve. The tax rate is the price of realizing a dollar of capital gains. Suppose that the realization function can be represented as a continuous curve, as in figure E-1. The welfare gain to individuals from a cut in tax rates is approximately equal to the sum of the windfall to individuals on the gains that would have been realized even at the higher tax rate, also known as the static revenue loss (area A on figure E-1), plus the additional triangle (B).[1] The triangle reflects the fact that some of the realizations induced by the lower tax rate would have occurred even if the tax cut had been smaller. The difference between the highest tax rate at which the new gains would be realized and the new tax rate is a gain to individuals. The sum of all these inframarginal gains is area B.

The Department of the Treasury's Office of Tax Analysis and, until 1994, the Joint Committee on Taxation approximated the benefit of tax reduction as the static revenue loss (area A).[2] For a small tax cut, this approximation is a good one. The area of B may be written as

Figure E-1. Realizations versus Tax Rate

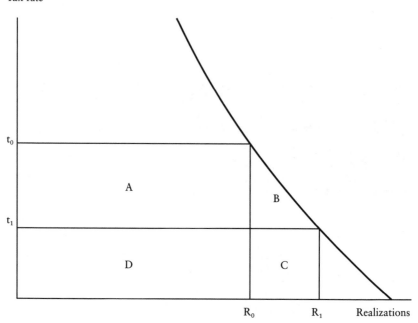

$$B \approx \frac{1}{2} A\epsilon \frac{\Delta t}{t},$$

where ϵ is the absolute value of the elasticity of realizations with respect to the tax rate, t is the tax rate, and Δt is the change in the tax rate.

The 1997 act cut tax rates on capital gains by about 30 percent for most taxpayers ($\Delta t/t = 0.30$). Using the elasticity estimate of about 0.3, the static revenue loss underestimates the welfare gain by less than 5 percent (½ times 0.3 times 0.3).[3] If capital gains were very responsive, so $\epsilon = 1$, the error would be about 15 percent. The important points are (1) the static revenue loss *understates* the gain to taxpayers of cutting rates and (2) the amount of understatement grows with the elasticity and the size of the tax cut.

The Joint Committee on Taxation no longer uses this method for distributing the benefits of capital gains tax cuts. It now uses the change in taxes paid to measure the benefit. In the context of figure E-1, this measure is $A - C$ (that is, $(D + C) - (A + D)$). For this method to accurately reflect the benefits to individuals of a tax cut, it would have to be true that the static revenue loss overestimates the welfare gain and that the amount of overstatement increases with the elasticity (because the size of C is largest when realizations are elastic). Of course, exactly the opposite is true. Thus, the JCT methodology vastly understates the benefit to people with capital gains of cutting the rate. If $\epsilon = 1.0$ and the tax change is small, then $C = A$, which means that there is no change in taxes paid. In this case, taxpayers with gains are calculated to get no benefit from a cut in tax rates, even though the gain is *larger* than the static estimate by $\frac{1}{2}\Delta t/t$.[4] If the elasticity were larger still, the tax cut would actually be scored as making people with gains worse off.[5]

Put another way, an elasticity greater than 1 would result in distribution tables showing people with gains to be better off when the tax rate increases. It is hard to imagine that they would agree with this conclusion. The JCT would counter that its distributional tables are not measures of well-being, but simply distributions of taxes paid, but distributional tables are inevitably interpreted as measures of tax burden. By that score, the JCT methodology is very misleading.

NOTES

Chapter 1

1. President George Bush, State of the Union, January 28, 1992.

2. Robert J. McIntyre, "Capital Gains Tax Cut: Bush Says 'Jobs, Jobs, Jobs' But History Says 'No, No, No.'" Press release, Citizens for Tax Justice, February 10, 1992.

3. Actually, a majority in Congress seemed to favor a capital gains tax cut, but Senate Majority Leader George Mitchell refused to allow the bill to come to the floor for a vote. See Michael J. Graetz, *The Decline [and Fall?] of the Income Tax* (New York: W. W. Norton, 1997). Graetz's chapter on capital gains is titled "The Madness of Two Georges" (Bush and Mitchell).

4. See, for example, Martin Feldstein, Joel Slemrod, and Shlomo Yitzhaki, "The Effects of Taxation on the Selling of Corporate Stock and the Realization of Capital Gains," *Quarterly Journal of Economics,* vol. 94, no. 4 (1980).

5. U.S. Department of the Treasury, *Report of the Department of the Treasury on Integration of the Individual and Corporate Tax Systems: Taxing Business Income Once* (Washington, D.C.: U.S. Government Printing Office, January 1992).

6. U.S. Congressional Budget Office, "Perspectives on the Ownership of Capital Assets and the Realization of Capital Gains," CBO Paper (May 1997).

Chapter 2

1. Jane Gravelle, *Capital Gains Tax Issues and Proposals: An Overview,* Congressional Research Service Report 95-64S (March 28, 1995).

2. A *capital asset* is property other than business inventory; property primarily held for sale to customers; a note or account receivable acquired in the ordinary

course of trade or business; a copyright or literary, musical, or artistic composition held by its creator (see Section 1221 of the Internal Revenue Code). Technically, depreciable assets and business real estate are not capital assets, but they can incur a capital gain or loss upon sale under certain conditions. See appendix A for details.

3. There are exceptions to the realization principle. Stock brokers, for example, are taxed on an accrual basis because the sale of shares is a normal part of a broker's trade or business. To deter abuse, the tax law also deems realization to have occurred in certain cases even though an asset has not technically been sold.

4. This paragraph draws heavily on Lawrence H. Seltzer, Selma F. Goldsmith, and M. Slade Kendrick, *The Nature and Tax Treatment of Capital Gains and Losses* (New York: National Bureau of Economic Research, 1951).

5. See Seltzer and others, *The Nature and Tax Treatment of Capital Gains and Losses.*

6. Charles C. Holt and John P. Shelton, "The Lock-In Effect of the Capital Gains Tax," *National Tax Journal*, vol. 15 (December 1962), pp. 337–52.

7. The 1997 law created an intermediate tax rate of 28 percent for assets held twelve to eighteen months. This significant source of complexity was eliminated by the 1998 act.

8. The AMT is a separate tax system designed to guarantee that taxpayers with high incomes do not use tax preferences to shelter a large share of their income from tax. Taxpayers must compute their tax liability under the AMT, compare it to their liability under the ordinary income tax, and pay whichever amount is greater. Since the AMT tax rates are higher than the maximum tax rates on long-term capital gains, taxpayers must repeat the separate tax calculations for each holding period to compute AMT tax liability.

9. Certain kinds of capital gains, such as those on installment sales, depreciable assets, and home sales are also reported on other forms. See the instructions to Schedule D in appendix A.

10. Thomas A. Barthold, Thomas Koerner, and John Navratil, "Effective Marginal Tax Rates under the Federal Individual Income Tax: Death by One Thousand Pin Pricks?" *National Tax Journal*, vol. 51 (September 1998), pp. 553–67.

11. For a discussion of some of the factors leading to the failure of this experiment, see Daniel Halperin, "Saving the Income Tax: An Agenda for Research," *Tax Notes*, vol. 77 (November 24, 1997), pp. 967–77.

12. This nickname was coined by Michael Kinsley (writing as "TRB"), "Angel of Death Loophole," *The New Republic*, July 13, 1997, p. 4.

13. Despite the loss limitation, taxpayers may still carefully time their realization of gains and losses to minimize their capital gains tax liability while realizing substantial amounts of cash from sales. See James M. Poterba, "How Burdensome Are Capital Gains Taxes?" *Journal of Public Economics*, vol. 33 (July

1987), pp. 157–72; or Alan J. Auerbach, Leonard E. Burman, and Jonathan Siegel, "Capital Gains Taxation and Tax Avoidance: New Evidence from Panel Data," in Joel Slemrod, ed., "Does Atlas Shrug? The Economic Consequences of Taxing the Rich," manuscript, 1997.

14. Note that 22 percent is the 38 percent rate reduced by the exclusion: $0.22 = 0.38 (1 - 0.44)$.

15. *Tax Reform Act of 1986: Report of the Committee on Finance United States Senate to Accompany H.R. 3838*, S. Rept. 99-313, 99 Cong. 2 sess.

16. Jeffrey H. Birnbaum and Alan S. Murray, *Showdown at Gucci Gulch* (New York: Random House, 1987).

17. Gravelle, *Capital Gains Tax Issues and Proposals*.

18. Gains of qualifying small business corporations are thought to be a very small fraction of total gains. Their exact size is unknown because the first sales under the provision will be for tax year 1998.

19. In addition to Australia and the United Kingdom, Iceland, Ireland, and Spain index capital gains for inflation. See Organization for Economic Cooperation and Development (OECD), *Taxing Profits in a Global Economy: Domestic and International Issues* (Paris: OECD, 1991).

20. OECD, *Taxing Profits in a Global Economy*.

21. New Hampshire and Tennessee have income taxes that apply only to interest and dividends.

22. William T. Bogart and William M. Gentry, "Capital Gains Taxes and Realizations: Evidence from Interstate Comparisons," *Review of Economics and Statistics*, vol. 77 (May 1995), pp. 267–82.

Chapter 3

1. Calculation based on data reported in Leonard E. Burman, Sally Wallace, and David Weiner, "How Capital Gains Taxes Distort Homeowners' Decisions," *National Tax Association Proceedings of the 89th Annual Conference on Taxation* (Washington, D.C., 1997), pp. 355–63.

2. TRA97 subjected such gains to a special 25 percent rate. The lower 20 percent rate applies only to the excess, if any, of the sale price over the purchase price (before adjusting for depreciation deductions).

Chapter 4

1. William Niskanen, "Analyzing the Budget Deal," interview with Margaret Warner, *News Hour with Jim Lehrer*, Public Broadcasting Service, July 29, 1997.

2. The practical argument for indexing is less clear-cut because of the complexity that indexing would introduce into the income tax. See Reed Shuldiner,

"Indexing the Tax Code," *Tax Law Review*, vol. 48 (1993), pp. 617–41; and C. Eugene Steuerle, *Taxes, Loans, and Inflation: How the Nations's Wealth Becomes Misallocated* (Brookings, 1985).

3. All dollar amounts and percentages reported here are rounded. Numbers in the computations were unrounded.

4. Jane C. Gravelle, *Limit to Capital Gains Feedback Effects,* Congressional Research Service Report for Congress 91-250RCO (March 1991).

5. See, for example, George M. Constantinides, "Optimal Stock Trading with Personal Taxes: Implications for Prices and the Abnormal January Returns," *Journal of Financial Economics,* vol. 13 (March 1984), pp. 65–89. Tax avoidance strategies are discussed later in the chapter.

6. Alan J. Auerbach, Leonard E. Burman, and Jonathan Siegel, "Capital Gains Taxation and Tax Avoidance: New Evidence from Panel Data," in Joel Slemrod, ed., "Does Atlas Shrug? The Economic Consequences of Taxing the Rich," manuscript, 1997.

7. Suppose a taxpayer has $100,000 in current losses and is considering whether to realize a $50,000 capital gain. She can do it tax-free in the current year, but she will have $50,000 less in carried-over losses to shelter future gains from tax. Assuming that she expects to realize a big gain next year unsheltered by losses, her taxable income will be $50,000 higher next year if she realizes the big gain this year. Thus the tax is simply deferred for a year, not avoided.

8. Auerbach and others, "Capital Gains Taxation and Tax Avoidance."

9. See R. Glenn Hubbard and Jonathan S. Skinner, "Assessing the Effectiveness of Saving Incentives," *Journal of Economic Perspectives,* vol. 10 (Fall 1996), pp. 73–90. Hubbard and Skinner suggest a cost-benefit analysis, where the cost includes the excess burden created by higher taxes and the benefit is the amount of savings induced by the tax subsidy. Under this criterion, a tax incentive that induced just enough private saving to offset the lost tax revenue would fail because of the substantial excess burden of distorting taxes.

10. The calculation is based on the way in which an exclusion would affect the returns from different types of investments and the shares of those types in total investment. See U.S. Congressional Budget Office, *Effects of Lower Capital Gains Taxes on Economic Growth,* CBO Paper (August 1990). These estimates are consistent with the cost of capital estimates in Steven M. Fazzari and Benjamin Herzon, "Capital Gains Taxes and Economic Growth," Public Policy Brief 25/1996 (Jerome Levy Economics Institute of Bard College, April 1996).

11. $2 \times 1.02 = 2.04$; $2 \times 1.035 = 2.07$.

12. See Douglas W. Elmendorf, *The Effect of Interest-Rate Changes on Household Saving and Consumption: A Survey,* Federal Reserve Board Working Paper 1996-27 (June 1996).

13. See Gravelle, *The Economic Effects of Taxing Capital Income.*

14. For a more technical explanation of how equilibrium saving and investment respond to rates of return, see appendix B.

15. See Joseph E. Stiglitz, "Some Aspects of the Taxation of Capital Gains," *Journal of Public Economics,* vol. 21 (June 1983), pp. 257–94.

16. See Constantinides, "Optimal Stock Trading with Personal Taxes"; Yves Balcer and Kenneth L. Judd, "Effects of Capital Gains Taxation on Life-Cycle Investment and Portfolio Management," *Journal of Finance,* vol. 42 (July 1987), pp. 743–58; and Diana B. Henriques and Floyd Norris, "Wealthy Helped by Wall St., Find New Ways to Escape Tax on Profits," *New York Times,* December 1, 1996, p. A1.

17. See Alan J. Auerbach, "Capital Gains Taxation in the United States: Realizations, Revenue and Rhetoric," *Brookings Papers on Economic Activity,* vol. 2 (1988), pp. 595–631; and Gravelle, *Limit to Capital Gains Feedback Effects.* These conclusions may be out of date, however. Recent accruals in the stock market have been much higher than the levels observed by Auerbach and Gravelle.

18. Economists also use elasticity to quantify other economic responses, such as how saving responds to changes in the rate of return (see appendix B). Elasticity is formally defined as the percentage change in one variable that results from a 1 percent change in another.

19. See Robert Gillingham and John S. Greenlees, "The Effect of Capital Gains Tax Rates on Capital Gains Tax Revenues: Another Look at the Evidence," *National Tax Journal,* vol. 45 (June 1992), pp. 167–77.

20. This problem is discussed later in the chapter.

21. See Leonard E. Burman, "A Theory of Aggregate Capital Gains Realizations," unpublished draft, Congressional Budget Office, May 1995; and Donald W. Kiefer, "Lock-in within a Simple Model of Corporate Stock Trading," *National Tax Journal,* vol. 43 (March 1990), pp. 75–94.

22. Gravelle, *Limits to Capital Gains Feedback Effects.*

23. For a critical review of the extensive literature on taxpayer responses to capital gains taxes, see George R. Zodrow, "Economic Analyses of Capital Gains Taxation: Realizations, Revenues, Efficiency and Equity," *Tax Law Review,* vol. 48 (1993), pp. 419–527.

24. Martin Feldstein, Joel Slemrod, and Shlomo Yitzhaki, "The Effects of Taxation on the Selling of Corporate Stock and the Realization of Capital Gains," *Quarterly Journal of Economics,* vol. 94 (1980), p. 785.

25. Leonard E. Burman, Kimberly A. Clausing, and John O'Hare, "Tax Reform and Realizations of Capital Gains in 1986," *National Tax Journal,* vol. 47 (March 1994), pp. 1–18.

26. Suppose an individual's tax rate in year s is defined as $T_{is} = \tau_{is} + \epsilon_{is}$ where τ_{is} is the permanent component and ϵ_{is} is the transitory (timing) component. Time-series regressions use

$$\overline{T}_{is} = \sum_{i=1}^{N} T_{is}/N$$

as an explanatory variable. Assuming the annual mean of $\epsilon_{is} = 0$, then

$$\overline{T}_{is} = \sum_{i=1}^{N} \tau_{is}/N.$$

That is, the aggregate average tax rate contains only the permanent component of individual tax rates.

27. This can also affect estimates from panel data to the extent that tax law changes affect different individuals differently. Because panel data include many observations for each year, the estimates can be computed controlling for the aggregate effect of tax law changes by the use of year dummies (fixed effects). William Shobe and Joel Slemrod ("The Tax Elasticity of Capital Gains Realizations: Evidence from a Panel of Taxpayers," Working Paper 3237 [Cambridge, Mass.: National Bureau of Economic Research, January 1990]) also controlled for individual fixed effects, thus removing the differential effects of tax law changes on individuals.

28. See Alan J. Auerbach, "Capital Gains Taxation and Tax Reform," *National Tax Journal*, vol. 42 (September 1989), pp. 391–401; Jonathan D. Jones, "An Analysis of Aggregate Time Series Capital Gains Equations," OTA Paper 65, Department of the Treasury (May 1989); and U.S. Congressional Budget Office, *How Capital Gains Tax Rates Affect Revenues: The Historical Evidence* (Washington, D.C.: GPO, 1988).

29. See Leonard E. Burman and William C. Randolph, "Measuring Permanent Responses to Capital Gains Tax Changes in Panel Data," *American Economic Review*, vol. 84 (September 1994), pp. 794–809. Their results are consistent with the findings of several others. Similar results covering the same period can be found in Shobe and Slemrod, "The Tax Elasticity of Capital Gains Realizations." Although Shobe and Slemrod were not able to measure permanent tax effects directly, when they controlled for fixed effects (which would include permanent tax effects), their estimates of transitory tax effects were consistent with the empirical findings of Burman and Randolph. For work that uses more recent data (for 1989), see Cathleen M. Koch, "The Response of Capital Gains Realizations to the 1986 Tax Reform Act," unpublished draft, Price Waterhouse (November 1994). For time-series data broken down by state and spanning a much longer time period, see William T. Bogart and William M. Gentry, "Capital Gains Taxes and Realizations: Evidence from Interstate Comparisons," *Review of Economics and Statistics*, vol. 77 (May 1995), pp. 267–82.

30. The point estimates for Burman and Randolph's preferred specification were 0.2 for the permanent elasticity and 6.4 for the transitory elasticity at 1982 tax rates. Although the permanent elasticity was not statistically significant, the difference in the elasticities was highly significant.

31. Chapter 5 discusses how tax shelters convert ordinary income into capital gains.

32. The maximum tax rate on capital gains (20 percent) is slightly more than half the top tax rate on ordinary income, which is 39.6 percent.

33. E. W. Cook and J. F. O'Hare, "Issues Relating to the Taxation of Capital Gains," *National Tax Journal,* vol. 15 (September 1987), pp. 473–88.

34. Although the parameter estimate reported by Cook and O'Hare in "Issues Relating to the Taxation of Capital Gains" is statistically significant, the authors do not state whether it is numerically large. That is, the authors do not indicate the extent to which induced realizations of capital gains are offset by reductions in interest and dividends. Their model also does not measure how interest expense responds to a capital gains differential.

35. Unpublished JCT estimate. The elasticity used by the Joint Committee on Taxation is significantly higher than that estimated by Burman and Randolph, "Measuring Permanent Responses to Capital Gains Tax Changes in Panel Data." Thus this calculation is likely to overstate the net effect on national saving and investment.

Chapter 5

1. See Patric H. Hendershott, Eric Toder, and Yunhi Won, "Effects of Capital Gains on Revenue and Economic Efficiency," *National Tax Journal,* vol. 44 (March 1991), pp. 21–40.

2. The effect is demonstrated theoretically by Daniel J. Kovenock and Michael Rothschild, "Capital Gains Taxation in an Economy with an 'Austrian Sector,'" *Journal of Public Economics,* vol. 21 (July 1983), pp. 215–56.

3. For further discussion of this particular effect, see Hendershott, Toder, and Won, "Effects of Capital Gains on Revenue and Economic Efficiency."

4. As discussed in chapter 4, that strategy was suggested by George M. Constantinides, "Optimal Stock Trading with Personal Taxes: Implications for Prices and the Abnormal January Returns," *Journal of Financial Economics,* vol. 13 (March 1984), pp. 65–89.

5. For a discussion of this and other techniques, see Diana B. Henriques and Floyd Norris, "Wealthy, Helped by Wall St., Find New Ways to Escape Tax on Profits," *New York Times,* December 1, 1996, p. A1.

6. See Fischer Black, "Noise," *Journal of Finance,* vol. 61 (July 1986), pp. 529–43.

7. A good survey of the evidence about investor myopia and noise trading can be found in Donald Kiefer, "Stock Market 'Short-Termism': Implications for Corporate Planning Horizons," *Congressional Research Service Report* 91-448RCO (May 29, 1991).

8. See Kiefer, "Stock Market 'Short-Termism.'"

9. This is the tax expenditure estimate for fiscal year 1998. See U.S. Office of Management and Budget, *Analytical Perspective: Budget of the United States Government, Fiscal Year 1998* (Washington, D.C.: GPO, 1998). The tax expenditure estimate does not account for behavioral responses, and so may under- or overestimate the revenue gain. Since taxing capital gains at death would have the effect of accelerating many realizations, the revenue gain in the short run would probably exceed the tax expenditure estimate.

10. On an investment that pays an uncertain return, which has before-tax variance s^2, the variance of after-tax return is $(1 - t)^2 s^2$, where t is the marginal tax rate on capital gains. The variance of a risky investment (that is, one with $s^2 > 0$) is lower when the tax rate is higher.

11. Agnar Sandmo, "The Effects of Taxation on Savings and Risk-Taking," in Alan J. Auerbach and Martin Feldstein, eds., *Handbook of Public Economics*, vol. 1 (Amsterdam: Elsevier B.V., 1985), p. 307.

12. For a formal demonstration that taxing capital gains may encourage risk-taking, see Martin S. Feldstein, "The Effect of Taxation on Risk-Taking," *Journal of Political Economy*, vol. 77 (September/October 1969), pp. 755–64.

13. This case must not be the norm, because the government collects substantial revenues from the tax on capital gains. Thus the "premium" must be less than actuarially fair on average.

14. See Alan J. Auerbach, Leonard E. Burman, and Jonathan Siegel, "Capital Gains Taxation and Tax Avoidance: New Evidence from Panel Data," in Joel Slemrod, ed., "Does Atlas Shrug? The Economic Consequences of Taxing the Rich," maunscript, 1997, fig. 3.

15. For a discussion, see Auerbach, Burman, and Siegel, "Capital Gains Taxation and Tax Avoidance."

16. Auerbach, Burman, and Siegel, "Capital Gains Taxation and Tax Avoidance."

17. U.S. Department of the Treasury, *Report to the Congress on the Capital Gains Tax Reductions of 1978* (Washington, D.C.: GPO, 1985); James M. Poterba, "Capital Gains Tax Policy toward Entrepreneurship," *National Tax Journal*, vol. 42 (September 1989), pp. 375–89.

18. Poterba, "Capital Gains Tax Policy toward Entrepreneurship," p. 375.

19. Jane G. Gravelle and Lawrence B. Lindsey, "Capital Gains," *Tax Notes*, vol. 38 (January 25, 1988), pp. 397–406.

20. See Kevin A. Hassett and R. Glenn Hubbard, "Tax Policy and Investment," in Alan J. Auerbach, ed., *Fiscal Policy: Lessons from Economic Research* (MIT Press, 1997). On the practical difficulties of indexing capital gains for inflation, see chapter 7.

21. Congress recognized this problem in 1997 when it decided to create a 25 percent tax rate for nonrecaptured capital gains on real estate. This rate is still

substantially lower than tax rates on ordinary income for high-income taxpayers, but it is higher than the rate that applies to long-term capital gains.

22. Leonard E. Burman, Thomas S. Neubig, and D. Gordon Wilson, "The Use and Abuse of Rental Project Models," in *Compendium of Tax Research: 1987* (Washington, D.C.: GPO, 1987).

23. Daniel Halperin, "Saving the Income Tax: An Agenda for Research," *Tax Notes*, vol. 77 (November 24, 1997), p. 970.

24. See strategies derived by Joseph E. Stiglitz, "Some Aspects of the Taxation of Capital Gains," *Journal of Public Economics*, vol. 21 (June 1983), pp. 257–94.

25. See the congressional testimony of Allen Sinai, *Capital Gains Tax Reduction and the Economy*, Hearings before the Senate Finance Committee on Capital Gains Tax Reduction, 105 Cong. 1 sess. (Washington, D.C.: GPO, March 13, 1997).

26. I tested lags up to five years against GDP growth. The strongest relationship was with a lag of four years, but even that was not statistically significant.

Chapter 6

Peter Ricoy collaborated on much of the material in this chapter. An earlier version was published as Leonard E. Burman and Peter Ricoy, "Capital Gains and the People Who Realize Them," *National Tax Journal*, vol. 50 (September 1997), pp. 427–51, and is reprinted with permission of the National Tax Association.

1. The index was at 970.43 in January 1998 compared with 466.51 in January 1994.

2. Even those numbers may be overstated. The tax revenue from capital gains is calculated by comparing actual income tax liability with what it would be if capital gains were zero. That is, capital gains are stacked last, after all other income. This procedure may overstate the importance of capital gains because of the progressivity of tax rates, especially in the years when a capital gains exclusion was in effect.

3. Shlomo Yitzhaki, "On the Relation between Return and Income," *Quarterly Journal of Economics*, vol. XX (February 1987), pp. 77–95.

4. For a detailed discussion of the data and additional tables, see U.S. Congressional Budget Office, "Perspectives on the Ownership of Capital Assets and the Realization of Capital Gains." CBO Paper (May 1997), appendix.

5. This terminology follows Joel Slemrod, "Taxation and Inequality: A Time-Exposure Perspective," in James M. Poterba, ed., *Tax Policy and the Economy*, vol. 6 (MIT Press, 1992). See also Michael Haliassos and Andrew B. Lyon, "Progressivity of Capital Gains Taxation with Optimal Portfolio Selection," in Joel Slemrod, ed., *Tax Progressivity and Income Inequality* (Cambridge University Press, 1994); and U.S. Department of the Treasury,

Report to the Congress on the Capital Gains Tax Reductions of 1978 (Washington, D.C.: GPO, 1985).

6. See Leonard E. Burman and Peter Ricoy, "Capital Gains and the People Who Realize Them," *National Tax Journal*, vol. 50 (September 1997), pp. 427–51.

7. Note that the tax data pertain to tax units—that is, individuals and families who file tax returns—whereas the data about wealth are based on families. Some families have multiple tax units, for example, because children have enough income that they are required to file separate returns.

8. In comparing the following figures, keep in mind that they reflect only data on tax returns. In particular, they exclude transfers from the government, such as food stamps, cash welfare payments, medicaid, and social security benefits.

9. Leonard E. Burman, Kimberly A. Clausing, and John O'Hare, "Tax Reform and Realizations of Capital Gains in 1986," *National Tax Journal,* vol. 47 (March 1994), pp. 1–18.

10. The details vary somewhat, depending on whether the tax return is for a single person or a married couple, and whether the taxpayer is older than sixty-four or not. Tabulations showing these differences are reported in the U.S. Congressional Budget Office, "Perspectives on the Ownership of Capital Assets and the Realization of Capital Gains," appendix.

11. See U.S. Congressional Budget Office, "Perspectives on the Ownership of Capital Assets and the Realization of Capital Gains," appendix.

12. David Bradford, quoted in Diana B. Henriques and Floyd Norris, "Wealthy, Helped by Wall St., Find New Ways to Escape Tax on Profits," *New York Times* December 1, 1996, p. A1.

13. For a discussion of the problem, see Alan J. Auerbach, Leonard E. Burman, and Jonathan Siegel, "Capital Gains Taxation and Tax Avoidance: New Evidence From Panel Data," in Joel S. Slemrod, ed., "Does Atlas Shrug? The Economic Consequences of Taxing the Rich," manuscript, 1997.

14. Burman, Clausing, and O'Hare, "Tax Reform and Realization of Capital Gains in 1986."

15. Leonard E. Burman and William C. Randolph, "Measuring Permanent Responses to Capital Gains Tax Changes in Panel Data," *American Economic Review,* vol. 84 (September 1994a), pp. 794–809.

16. George M. Constantinides, "Optimal Stock Trading with Personal Taxes: Implications for Prices and the Abnormal January Returns," *Journal of Financial Economics,* vol. 13 (March 1984), pp. 65–89.

17. James M. Poterba, "How Burdensome Are Capital Gains Taxes?" *Journal of Public Economics,* vol. 33 (July 1987), pp. 157–72.

18. Auerbach, Burman, and Siegel, "Capital Gains Taxation and Tax Avoidance."

19. Auerbach, Burman, and Siegel, "Capital Gains Taxation and Tax Avoidance."

20. Tables 6-9 and 6-10 are based on data for the Sales of Capital Assets study compiled by the IRS. They exclude bonds and transactions for which inflation factors could not be computed. About one-third of transactions lacked enough information to compute an inflation factor. See U.S. Congressional Budget Office, "Perspectives on the Ownership of Capital Assets and the Realization of Capital Gains," appendix.

21. The long boom in the stock market makes it unlikely that current data would show the same pattern.

22. Indexing capital gains for inflation is discussed in chapter 7.

23. Note that the indexing that exists under current law does not in any case adjust the measurement of income for inflation. Instead, it is designed so that tax schedules and phaseouts apply to the same levels of real income from year to year, for example, to avoid "bracket creep," that is, to avoid being pushed into higher tax brackets solely because of inflation.

24. The tax is the difference between the actual 1993 tax liability and the tax that would have been owed if no capital gains had been reported in 1993.

25. U.S. Joint Committee on Taxation, *Methodology and Issues in Measuring Changes in the Distribution of Tax Burdens* (Washington, D.C.: GPO, 1993).

26. This measure is only an approximation for several reasons. It does not account for interactions among tax provisions, especially with the alternative minimum tax. In addition, the tax cut in 1997 was structured as a set of maximum tax rates rather than a percentage cut in rates and had special rates for certain classes of assets. Nonetheless, the overall distribution of benefits from the 1997 tax reductions is likely to be similar to the distribution of taxes shown in table 6-11.

Chapter 7

1. For further discussion of the loss limit, see Leonard E. Burman and Eric J. Toder, "Indexing vs. Exclusion of Capital Gains: Effects on Income Distribution and Economic Efficiency," *NTA-TIA Proceedings of the 85th Annual Conference* (Columbus, Ohio: National Tax Association, 1992), pp. 10–18. Burman and Toder found that the special loss limit would have little direct effect on taxable gains—increasing them by less than 5 percent in 1985—although the effect might be larger now. But the main impetus for the indexing loss limit is to discourage the tax-sheltering response.

2. U.S. Congressional Budget Office, *Indexing Capital Gains* (Washington, D.C.: GPO, 1990).

3. Burman and Toder, "Indexing vs. Exclusion of Capital Gains."

4. Other alternatives to holding an asset are to sell to finance either current consumption or the purchase of an asset, such as a personal residence or a bond, that is unlikely to produce taxable capital gains. In both of these cases, an exclusion

reduces lock-in more than indexing. For a discussion, see Congressional Budget Office, *Capital Gains Taxes in the Short Run* (Washington, D.C.: GPO, 1991).

5. U.S. Congressional Budget Office, *Indexing Capital Gains.*

6. Reed Shuldiner, "Index the Code, Not Capital Gains," *Tax Notes,* vol. 79 (April 13, 1998), pp. 225–42, illustrates the problem of indexing capital gains while not indexing debt with the following example. Assume that an asset is fully debt-financed and the dividends paid on the asset exactly equal the interest payments. Any nominal gain or loss on disposition of the asset is pure profit, because the investment was costless (the dividends covered the interest). Nonetheless, under indexing, some or all of the profit would be excluded from tax depending on the inflation rate. That is, the investor's real after-tax profit would increase with inflation. Note that Shuldiner's argument applies with equal force when the investor sells a bond that would have paid interest at the same rate as the dividend yield for the asset. Again, the investor's increase in real wealth when the asset is sold is equal to the nominal capital gain.

7. Diana Furchtgott-Roth (American Enterprise Institute), interviewed by Kathleen Schalch on National Public Radio's *Morning Edition,* July 14, 1997.

8. See Burman and Toder, "Indexing vs. Exclusion of Capital Gains."

9. See Burman and Toder, "Indexing vs. Exclusion of Capital Gains." Note that the early 1980s were a much different environment for investments than the 1990s. Inflation was much higher and real returns on investments in the stock market were much smaller. Thus Burman and Toder's findings might not hold up in the face of more recent data.

10. Shuldiner, "Index the Code, Not Capital Gains."

11. Shuldiner, "Index the Code, Not Capital Gains."

12. U.S. Congressional Budget Office, *Indexing Capital Gains.*

13. According to the New York State Bar Association, the problems of avoidance and tax arbitrage under indexing could only be addressed through extremely complex laws and regulations, and for that reason it has recommended against indexation. See New York State Bar Association, Tax Section Ad Hoc Committee on Indexation of Basis, "Report on Inflation Adjustments to the Basis of Capital Assets," *Tax Notes,* vol. 48 (August 6, 1990), pp. 759–75. A similar conclusion was reached by Shuldiner in "Index the Code," but he also argues that indexing capital gains alone is unnecessary and inefficient.

Chapter 8

1. In practice, there are many variants of corporate tax integration. For a discussion of the role of the capital gains tax under various options for corporate tax integration, see U.S. Department of the Treasury, *Report of the Department of the Treasury on Integration of the Individual and Corporate Tax Systems: Taxing Business Income Once* (Washington, D.C.: GPO, January 1992), chap. 8.

2. In 1995 only 1.2 percent of taxpayers were in the 36 or 39.6 percent brackets. Leonard E. Burman, William Gale, and David Weiner, "Six Tax Laws Later: How Individuals' Marginal Federal Income Tax Rates Changed between 1980 and 1995," *National Tax Journal,* vol. 51 (September 1998), pp. 637–52.

3. Kevin Hassett emphasized this point to me in personal conversation.

4. Estimates are based on data in tables 6-7 and 6-11.

5. Leonard E. Burman, Sally Wallace, and David Weiner, "How Capital Gains Taxes Distort Homeowners' Decisions," *National Tax Association Proceedings of the 89th Annual Conference on Taxation* (Washington, D.C.: National Tax Association, 1997), pp. 355–63.

6. For the efficiency cost of housing tax subsidies, see also Todd Sinai, "Taxation, Mobility, and Demand for Owner-Occupied Housing," paper prepared for the National Tax Association Symposium (Washington, D.C., 1996).

7. The housing rollover provision had one drawback that would not apply to corporate stock, for example. People who purchased larger houses than they would have preferred wasted real economic resources as a result of their excess, because housing consumption is tied directly to the amount of investment.

8. See William Vickrey, "Averaging Income for Income Tax Purposes," *Journal of Political Economy,* vol. 47 (June 1939), pp. 379–97.

9. For a demonstration, see Alan J. Auerbach, "Retrospective Capital Gains Taxation," *American Economic Review,* vol. 81 (March 1991), pp. 167–78.

10. Auerbach, "Retrospective Capital Gains Taxation."

11. The imputed basis is $1/1.06^{10}(\$10,000) = \$5,584$.

12. Family farms and businesses receive preferential treatment under the estate tax, so the definition for purposes of calculating capital gain at death could conform to the definition under the estate tax.

13. For more information, see Congressional Budget Office, *Capital Gains Taxes in the Short Run* (Washington, D.C.: GPO, 1991).

14. U.S. Congressional Budget Office, *Capital Gains Taxes in the Short Run.*

15. U.S. Congressional Budget Office, *How Capital Gains Tax Rates Affect Revenues: The Historical Evidence* (Washington, D.C.: GPO, 1988).

Chapter 9

1. See the argument of self-avowed supply-sider Fleming Saunders, "The Investor Who Worked Too Hard: Capital Gains and Ordinary Income Should Have Same Low Tax Rate," *Tax Notes,* vol. 81 (November 2, 1998), pp. 655–62.

2. U.S. Department of the Treasury, *Tax Reform for Fairness, Simplicity, and Economic Growth* (Washington, D.C.: GPO, 1984).

3. Capital gains would still retain an advantage because they can be deferred until realization, but with gains fully taxed upon realization or at death, the value of deferral would diminish significantly.

4. Daniel Halperin, "Saving the Income Tax: An Agenda for Research," *Tax Notes*, vol. 77 (November 24, 1997), pp. 967–77.

5. See Jane G. Gravelle and Lawrence B. Lindsey, "Capital Gains," *Tax Notes*, vol. 38 (January 25, 1988), pp. 397–406.

6. This phenomenon is observable around the "ex-dividend" date. Shares of stock purchased after a certain date each quarter—the ex-dividend date—do not receive a dividend; the owner of record at the ex-dividend date receives it. As a result, stock prices fall by the amount of the dividend.

Appendix C

1. An earlier version of this appendix appeared as Leonard E. Burman and William C. Randolph, "Measuring Permanent Responses to Capital Gains Tax Changes in Panel Data," Department of the Treasury, *OTA Paper* 68 (August 1994).

2. The sample used to construct figure C-1 includes only taxpayers who realized net positive long-term capital gains at least once between 1979 and 1983. The first-dollar tax rate is the marginal tax rate on the first dollar of long-term capital gains, that is, computed with capital gains set to zero.

3. By comparing quartiles of conditional distributions to percentiles of the unconditional distributions, we have deliberately abstracted from intertemporal variations that would have resulted from general shifts in the marginal tax-rate schedule due, for example, to statutory changes in marginal tax rates in 1981 and 1982. As a result, figure C-1 provides a better picture of the degree to which dispersion of marginal tax rates in a cross-sectional sample results from intertemporal variation because general shifts that are not represented by the figure would not result in cross-sectional variation in tax rates.

Appendix E

1. This analysis make several simplifying assumptions: first, that taxes are levied at a fixed rate, and second, that individuals' realizations are a continuous function of the tax rate. The assumptions are unlikely to change the qualitative conclusions.

2. Jane G. Gravelle, *Distributional Effects of the Proposed Tax Cut*, Congressional Research Service Report for Congress 97-669E (July 2, 1997).

3. This elasticity estimate is from Leonard E. Burman and William C. Randolph, "Measuring Permanent Responses to Capital Gains Tax Changes in Panel Data," *American Economic Review*, vol. 84 (September 1994), pp. 794–809.

4. The Joint Committee on Taxation staff made many of these points in their 1993 brochure: "The increased taxes paid as a result of increased realizations is not an increase in tax burden. . . . Because calculating tax benefit on induced real-

izations is very difficult and because the benefit is likely to be small, the JCT staff ignores this benefit and distributes only the change in tax burden that would have been realized in the absence of the tax cut. This convention has the effect, however, of underestimating the benefits of a tax cut on capital gains income." U.S. Joint Committee on Taxation, *Methodology and Issues in Measuring Changes in the Distribution of Tax Burdens* (Washington, D.C.: GPO, 1993), pp. 46–47.

5. In fact, tables prepared by the JCT show an increase in tax in the short run, when they assume an elasticity greater than 1.

INDEX